To Im ~~~

A 30-YEAR CYCLE

Get well soon
Enjoy my journey!

C.
August '13.

To Uncle Graham

Get well soon!
Enjoy in January!

Love,
August 16.

A 30-YEAR CYCLE

Chris Boulton

The Choir Press

Copyright © 2013 Chris Boulton

All rights reserved. No part of this publication may be reproduced or transmitted in any form or by any means, electronic or mechanical including photocopying, recording or any information storage or retrieval system, without prior permission in writing from the publishers.

The right of Chris Boulton to be identified as the author of this work has been asserted by him in accordance with the Copyright, Designs and Patents Act 1988

First published in the United Kingdom in 2013
by The Choir Press

ISBN 978-1-909300-13-2

For my dad – I miss your calls

Contents

Acknowledgements ix

Introduction 1
Tourmalet – a beginning but nearly the end 4
Straight to the heart of it 11
Back in the saddle 24
Setting the objective – relive my youth! 34
Racing again 51
Testing traditions 63
Old gits (retire immediately) 71
Things cyclists do 75
Heroes 88
The club time warp 90
Training then and now – power to the people 106
You are what you eat 120
Wow, that hurts 127
My dad, the directeur sportif 132
Family matters but it doesn't matter to family 139
Nearly there, nearly there 146
The end or a new beginning? 152

Postscript 155
Glossary 156

Acknowledgements

To my wife, Jennifer, for her support with the initial edit of this book but most of all for putting up with me during my sometimes tough road to recovery post-op and my 'obsession' with my cycling goals. My boys, Albert and Arthur, for giving me a reason to keep fit.

My editor, Harriet Evans, for her clear professional advice, efficiency and support during the editing process. Sally Jeans, my sister-in-law, for her attention to detail in reading through the proofs. Most welcomed and appreciated by me as a novice writer.

The Wayfarers Wheelers, Pete Dunmore, Simon Holland and Steve Suttie – thanks for your companionship over many miles together, long may this continue. Our sponsors for the Étape du Tour kit, Stuart Cameron (the happiest man on a bike) and Neil Leah, and my mum for her continued interest in what I get up to – Sunday mornings weren't all a waste of time!

I would also like to thank my coaches, Adrian Timmis and John Morgan, for their guidance and support but most of all for putting up with my moaning and stupid questions. My cardiologist, Dr Carl Brookes, for his clear advice and support. And finally my friends at Newbury Road Club: proof that the cycling club time warp does exist!

Introduction

This book was conceived very late one night, as time drifted on into the early hours of the morning. I was in a grubby and noisy motel in the lovely French town of Pau, nestling at the foothills of the Pyrenees. I couldn't sleep, tormented with failure. I agonised over my story, thinking about what I could do next, and posted the briefest of notes about it on Twitter. Would it be interesting? Could I articulate what I had been through and why? You can be the judge of that. But telling this story in my own way has proved cathartic.

This book is actually about the story of two periods in my life, 30 years apart. I called it *A 30-Year Cycle* because that is what I went through: a long journey back around to doing what I enjoyed in my youth. For some reason, which I am unable to put my finger on now, I left cycling alone after some limited success in the 1981 season. The many distractions of youth, starting working life and growing up were certainly the main causes and of course this is the route many young people follow, leaving their respective sports to do other things in life, some never to return. Many just get on and enjoy life without a sporting passion, at best getting involved vicariously, as a supporter, perhaps. There is nothing wrong with that, but I am someone who likes to immerse myself in my chosen sport and put up with the compromises in family life. Both times I have been involved with cycling,

A 30-YEAR CYCLE

at each end of my age spectrum, I have made it a big part of my life; that's the way I'm wired.

I hope my story will be of interest to all, but I guess it will especially interest cyclists, whatever they do in the sport and wherever they do it. In its essence, this book is partly about training for a particular event, specifically a 25-mile time trial, and maintains a focus on that, but it's also a commentary on how the sport was in the early eighties for a keen club rider and what has changed since then (very little in some areas!)

For those able to perform at a very much higher level in cycling or even other sports, their focus will have been on winning major events or breaking records. For me, it has just been about going 'under the hour' in a 25-mile time trial after a time lapse of 30 years. Not a great sporting feat, but still a benchmark for a keen cyclist and of course repeating something I had done a long time before with the advantage of youth and an untouched heart.

I wish I had been, but even as a youth, I wasn't a great cyclist, not really even a good one. As a teenager and into my early twenties, though, I was good enough to be competitive at club level and always had hope. Thirty years on, all I have done is strive to be the same. At first I thought it wasn't possible, but slowly I turned my performances around. Many people helped. Some in an outwardly positive way: my coaches, for instance. Others by being deeply negative, or even by showing no interest at all, often questioning what the point was, actually made a substantially more positive impact. They drove me on, sometimes, out of anger, because I knew they were wrong or just, in some cases, because they didn't get the point of achieving anything in a sporting sense.

I also hope this book will interest those who have had

Introduction

heart problems or any health issues, who have got on with life, not accepting any limitations of a particular affliction, and achieved something they really wanted to, especially if others said they couldn't. To those of you out there who have a challenge, no matter how great or small, perhaps my story might be an inspiration to you. In the summer of 2012 the world watched the events at the London 2012 Paralympic Games. The athletes there were a total inspiration, overcoming far greater challenges and achieving more than I ever will. I have total respect for them and feel very humble about my own quest when, in some cases, they have overcome overwhelming odds to succeed.

My tale is not meant to impress but sometimes to amuse, certainly to be of interest and hopefully to uplift. I worked hard and used the better equipment available through nearly 30 years of technical advances and also much improved training methods to help achieve my goal. I had to take advantage of these anyway for no other reason than that I didn't have the time to train any other way. It took grit and determination and almost became an obsession. As my cardiologist once said, while encouraging me to write this book, 'Most people with a prosthetic heart valve lead a sedentary life, but you aren't one of them, are you?' I think you know what I said!

Tourmalet – a beginning but nearly the end

Lower slopes of the Tourmalet, Sunday 18th July 2010. There were ten kilometres to go. The heat was unbearable; sweat poured out of me. All the noise around me melted into the background. I felt faint and struggled to push the pedals around. My heart rate sat at 143 beats a minute although I was hardly moving. It had been a lot higher. I felt sick and lightheaded.

I wobbled a little and ran the risk of slipping down the rough edge at the side of the road into the drainage ditch.

I had lost sight of and contact with the others in my group of friends doing the Étape hours earlier and was all alone. This had never happened to me before. I was going to have to give up. Finally I did. I had almost literally ridden myself into the ground.

The relief was overwhelming and what energy I had left while I sat on my bike seemed to evaporate when I got off. I couldn't stand; my legs just buckled. Using my bike as a support, I staggered across the road and sat on a low wall in the limited shade at the side of the gently rising slope, the tarmac slowly melting in the early afternoon heat. Then I started to throw up; it just kept coming . . .

The very efficient and friendly but totally impersonal guys who ripped my number off and took my bike away

Tourmalet – a beginning but nearly the end

were kind and seemed concerned. Did I want a doctor? Maybe I did, but my pride made me respond reflexively with a 'Non'. They left me alone to wait for the bus and I didn't care; I felt completely at peace and totally knackered. I thought how selfish I was for pushing myself so hard. My family at home would be waiting to hear how I had got on and would be very worried to hear about the state I was now in.

I then waited for what seemed like an eternity to be picked up by the bus for the slow, shameful journey up the twisting road to the Tourmalet summit and the finish line. Even more shameful for me, I had to sit on the step facing out of the open door, puking, as the bus crawled up the mountain. The regurgitated mix of gels and isotonic fluid seemed to be never-ending. I thought that surely, I couldn't be sick for much longer. When I had got in the bus I had felt a little better. I had been greeted not by a bunch of losers but by some fit-looking guys with deep tans, chatting away in various languages pretty cheerfully. Wow, I had thought, if these guys couldn't finish then I had stood no chance. But the need to deal with my sickness had put paid to a brief emotional boost.

After what seemed like hours twisting and turning up the Tourmalet, passing cyclists wobbling along on their bikes, walking or just sitting at the roadside in their own personal defeat, we finally reached the cool mountain air of the summit. I hoped the others would be there but soon realised I wouldn't find them. It was so busy with people milling around clutching their Étape finishers' medals with glee and others, just like me, seeking repatriation with their bikes. Total chaos at 2,115 metres (6,939 feet.) Luckily for me it was still warm and dry; if it had been cold and wet I think I would have been an ambulance case.

A 30-YEAR CYCLE

I couldn't find anything to eat or drink and felt dehydrated and very sick. I knew I had to get my bike off one of the trucks and cycle down to the village of La Mongie. It took well over an hour before I was sitting back in the saddle and heading downhill to the agreed rendezvous point at the Laurent Fignon Centre. The journey seemed interminable and so dangerous due to the traffic. There was a steady queue of cars trying to get down the mountain and cars also coming along very fast in the uphill direction in the growing dusk. I was past caring and just pressed on, cycling in the middle of the road; all I wanted to do was get this over with. What could have been a pleasant evening ride in the mountains, with the afterglow of a good event, was more like a miserable, keep-your-wits-about-you commute in busy London traffic.

When I finally rolled into the car park at the Laurent Fignon Centre the relief was overwhelming. My immediate feelings were that I would never ride a bike again, but this would soon subside. I had to focus on locating my bike box and packing my bike away for the journey home. It was yet another scene of complete chaos, bike boxes, bikes and weary riders strewn all over the grassy area to the front of the Centre. I found my box and set about sorting out my bike. It would have been nice to have just left it there but common sense prevailed; I knew I would need it again!

The others had obviously been there for some time and had nearly finished packing their bikes away. Despite the fact they had all completed the event (just), the atmosphere was strangely subdued and none of them wanted to talk. Looking back, I think it was because they didn't know what to say to me, the organiser and motivator for the trip, knowing they had

Not happy! – Col du Soulor, 2010 l'Etape de Tour.

succeeded where I had failed. I like to think I would have been far more communicative and supportive if it had been the other way around. The awkward silence really made it worse for me, even more so when, having finished with sorting their bikes, they left me alone and went in for a meal. I finally got to join them but sadly the atmosphere was still flat. I think that probably the exhaustion and relief at the end of a long day were overwhelming.

After leaving La Mongie we faced a long bus journey back to Pau. I slept on and off in the uncomfortable seat all the way back to our motel, completely exhausted; it wasn't until we had arrived there and I lay in bed that night, nearly 20 hours after leaving on the day's nightmare journey, that the seeds for this story began to germinate. The thing that really got to me was failure, especially while doing something I had really wanted to do and I enjoyed so much. I didn't really know why I had been forced to climb off my bike with just 10 km to go, although I thought it was probably a mixture of my reduced aerobic capacity and sunstroke which accounted for the sickness. I assume the cocktail of isotonic drinks I had taken also hadn't helped.

After my return to the UK I thought long and hard about what I should do. Should I give up riding a bike again and admit defeat on all sporting endeavours? After all, I had given the London Marathon another try the year before and that had been an unmitigated disaster. I had felt so crap from about 13 miles that it had become a 'mind over matter' experience finishing in an almost delirious state, in an embarrassing time of over five hours.

I had trained hard for the Marathon and for the Étape but all my efforts just hadn't worked for me. I had some

Tourmalet – a beginning but nearly the end

nagging doubts about my heart after the Tourmalet experience and, bowing to pressure from my wife and parents, went to see my cardiologist, just for a check-up. I was pleasantly surprised and immensely relieved to get a clean bill of health and actually positive encouragement from him. He was sympathetic about my poor performance and taking on board my heart issues, although I hadn't finished the Étape he seemed impressed with what I had achieved. He knew I was clearly very slow riding uphill but was amazed I could ride a bike at over 20 mph on the flat! Little did he know that wasn't fast at all to serious cyclists and what I was thinking about needed me to be able to ride at well over 25 mph.

I soon made a decision, based on my night-time thoughts after the Étape. I needed something else to test me. Bearing in mind I didn't enjoy 'gentle' or aimless rides around the countryside, even sportives and the like, I resolved to get back into racing. I knew it couldn't be road racing, where all my real passion for the sport lay. I just hadn't been able to keep up or cope with the frequent changes of pace when I had tried a road race the previous year. It was racing against the clock in the form of time trials that became the only option. I had tried a few as training for the Étape and enjoyed them, although my performances were very slow and compared to my peers incredibly poor. On the positive side, those performances were anonymous.

The autumn came; I kept on riding and actually improving slightly. Then, after a brief break off the bike, I started training in earnest in a structured way, the first time I had done so on a bike, at any rate, for 30 years. Getting back into a training regime was amazingly easy for me. I am an organised person and like structure. I am

A 30-YEAR CYCLE

also very able to stick to a plan given the right objective, almost to the point of obsession, although my wife believes it has gone well beyond that!

Straight to the heart of it

In 1997 I decided I wanted to learn to fly. Why? Well, it was a childhood dream; I finally had the time to do it and more importantly the money. All progressed well and within six or so short hours my flying instructor, Vic, told me to get a medical certificate. That could only mean one thing, I thought; flying solo for the first time was on the cards ...

I set about making an appointment for a medical with an aeromedical examiner in Harley Street, near where I worked. I have to admit, there was a nagging doubt about whether I would pass based on the fact that ten years or so before, when I was planning to join the Army, a doctor had found a heart murmur. It was described to me at the time as 'nothing to worry about' and I was passed fit for military service. At the end of one detailed examination, the Army doctor did say 'it might cause problems in later life' but that was it! Off I went, fit for the Army. I didn't really think about it again.

I kept on reassuring myself that the doubt I felt was no more than the normal anxiety people experience when going for any form of medical examination. After all, it is completely natural to worry about what might be found. In any case, my confidence was also bolstered by the results of a company medical I had undergone a couple of months earlier when the doctor concerned had told me that the heart murmur, when listened to via a stetho-

A 30-YEAR CYCLE

scope, sounded no different than it had two years earlier and was 'nothing to worry about'.

Anyway, I attended the medical and, compounding my worst fears, the examiner told me at the end that he wouldn't be able to give me a certificate. What he went on to say was very worrying.

'I don't like the sound of your murmur; you need to go for some tests, just to be sure.'

He probably never knew, but I am pretty certain his concern that day and his recommendation saved my life!

People often ask if I had any symptoms that might have suggested my heart murmur was more serious; chest pain, breathlessness or something else connected with heart problems. I hadn't noticed anything that affected my everyday life. Looking back, though, it became obvious to me something had been wrong. I used to run regularly on my own and had gradually noticed it was becoming harder. I put this down to age and not getting out to train enough. When I ran with others I had become noticeably slower – I remember running in Hyde Park a few lunchtimes with work colleagues and not being able to keep up. It hadn't been an issue before, but again I put this down to the young guns in the office forcing the pace.

I had also taken part for a few years in an event called the Karrimor International Mountain Marathon or KIMM for short. This is basically a two-day, long-distance orienteering event. That autumn I had taken part again in a two-man team and boy, did I suffer. It was always a hard event, especially due to the distance to be covered, often in inclement weather, and the mountainous terrain. I wasn't able to get going and just had to dig deeper and deeper to keep up with my teammate, Mark. I was always a few paces or more behind him and, bearing in

Straight to the heart of it

mind it was me doing the navigation, you can imagine the difficulties this created. We finished but with a very mediocre time and low overall score.

I just didn't like admitting defeat and would often push myself on out of sheer frustration or embarrassment at being left behind by my peers. This was probably quite a dangerous thing to do.

To cut a long story short, although things progressed slowly with various tests over a two-month period, I knew I probably had a serious problem with my heart. During this time I even kept on running until a very shocked doctor said stop! In the end, I had open heart surgery to replace my mitral valve in February 1998.

Knowing I had to have open heart surgery was weird. Life was in effect put on hold. I couldn't commit to things. For the first time in years I had no adventures planned for the coming year. In my state of mind I made some strange decisions. I even got rid of my car; my company car lease had come to an end and in view of the operation and the recovery period following I decided to leave taking a new one on until I was ready. It felt like my life would become one of two halves: that before the operation and that afterwards. I really didn't have any idea of what life would be like after 18th February 1998.

The night before my operation I was all alone lying on the bed and deep in thought. There was a knock at the door and in walked a nurse with a razor.

'Need to shave your chest,' she said.

'Do I have a choice?'

A few minutes later there I was smooth-chested, looking like a plucked chicken and painted with iodine.

The 'nil by mouth' sign was put on the door and I felt like the condemned man waiting for his fate. I had a fitful

A 30-YEAR CYCLE

night's sleep but was amazingly pretty calm. I was woken up very early the next day due to the sunlight streaming through the window. All I could do was wait. A nurse came in with a surgical gown and I dutifully put it on and then craved breakfast, but none came; I always wake up ravenous but all that I was allowed was a cup of pre-med. Luckily the wait wasn't too long and soon after two cheery porters arrived and off I went to theatre.

'Small scratch,' said my surgeon ...

I woke up in intensive care some time later; I just don't know when. I immediately threw up and continued doing so. The whole thing was very unpleasant but there was no pain. I was given a towelling pad to hold against my chest when I retched. I was convinced my aching rib cage would burst apart and the pad offered some comfort when pressed hard against it.

I have often suffered from migraine headaches; they usually start with visual effects. These can be a rippling distortion of my eyesight, jagged streaks of light, blind spots or tunnel vision. I started to get some effects and thought *oh no*, but for the first time there was no headache. I assume the strong painkillers I was on stopped that.

The only weirdly pleasant thing I remember was the fact I had been left with a catheter inserted into my bladder which effortlessly drained away my pee as I lay there. Strange, I know, but true. I did wonder just who had inserted the tube into my penis and hoped it was the good-looking nurse who had been tending me since I had woken up. Then I thought perhaps it would be better if she hadn't; it wouldn't have been in its best form!

I was wired up and had numerous drips inserted into

my neck and arms. The ones in my neck kept on coming out as I moved. I also noticed a tube and a wire coming out of my torso. The tube was a drain left in after the op. I found out later the wire was called a 'pacing wire'. I never asked how it might have been used but always assumed it was there in case my heart stopped!

Both the wire and the tube were removed a few days later.

'Wiggle your toes,' said the nurse.

I did, and the wire was quickly pulled out before I could even say 'ouch!'

I was soon moved from intensive care to a shared room. I have already mentioned my migraines; one had come on soon after waking up from my operation. That had been 'masked' by the painkillers. I was expecting more painful headaches but surprisingly didn't suffer another one during my whole stay in hospital although at times it was quite stressful.

The Wellington Hospital in St John's Wood, London, was a fairly pleasant place for a medical institution. But it was so bloody noisy! Even in the middle of the night there were comings and goings and also at times I had to put up with another patient sharing my room. The first was a very nervous guy who rather annoyingly paced around; I would have too if I had been him. He appeared on the night before an operation to remove part of his lung. He was or at least had been, by his own admission, a heavy smoker, so I could imagine what ailment he may have had.

My next roommate was a really nice Jewish guy; I never got an inkling of what was wrong with him. It may have all been a sham to get away from his matriarchal and domineering wife. She kept on turning up and nagging him continuously about anything and pretty much everything. I felt very sorry for him at times; he was scheduled to leave more than once and for whatever reason the doctors kept him in at the last minute.

The poor guy couldn't relax. It was either his wife giving him a hard time or something going wrong, usually with his kosher food. What should really have been a pretty simple service from the hospital catering team just became a desperate nightmare for him. Some days it just didn't arrive, he would get the same as me. Rather perversely, in view of the ongoing health of my heart, I had started to order the rather good full English breakfast, so clearly that wasn't right for him.

One morning he had been told it was a kosher breakfast that had been delivered. There he was tucking in next to me when all of a sudden a member of the catering staff came in with a tray wrapped in what looked like layers of cling film.

'Here's your kosher breakfast,' she said.

'What?' he spluttered, realising he was eating non-kosher food and spitting it out onto the tray.

I did find this funny and nearly choked on my sausage and bacon but afterwards felt full of remorse. Following his religious beliefs was clearly everything to him and it became a topic of conversation for him and various visitors for days to come. When I finally left hospital he was still there. Me being allowed out made him more miserable. I wished him luck, collected my things and moved back into the real world.

Two or so days after the operation, as I was relaxing in bed, the physiotherapist appeared. I knew who she was; we had met briefly the night before my surgery when she had promised to visit me afterwards.

Straight to the heart of it

'You're a bit young for this,' she had said, referring to me needing a heart valve replacement at the tender age of 35. She had then gone on to tell me more details about my operation; actually too much detail with a graphic description of how they would break my ribcage to get at my heart. I had switched off and hadn't really listened.

On our second meeting she was clearly going to take no messing around. I was asked to get out of bed, which I dutifully did, then I was told to walk. So I obeyed and walked, or rather shuffled, a few paces, using the edge of the bed to balance, before collapsing into a chair. The journey back into the bed felt like running a marathon.

A day or so later and I had made it as far as the lift. Down we went.

'Right, one flight today. To the top by the end of the week!'

'You're not serious,' I exclaimed as I struggled breathlessly up to the first half-landing, looking up between the stairs to the ten or twelve flights above.

It was a struggle too. I could hear my valve ticking, clearly working away, which was both comforting and alarming in equal measure, and was all in after two steps, the ticking in my chest getting louder. The remaining steps felt like I remembered climbing at high altitude: one step, catch your breath and then next step, and so on.

This torturous exercise went on for over a week and gradually with each day I made it up a few more steps. There became two things in my daily routine that I absolutely hated: the stair exercises and the blood test with the very nice lady from Portland, Oregon – I called her 'the vampire', which she thought was funny.

In the second week I managed to make it right from

the basement all the way to the top floor. It wasn't easy, but I could do it without feeling sick or faint. Overwhelming tiredness was a factor though. "What had become of me?" I thought. Pre-op I would have easily climbed the stairs even with my underlying condition. Now, I was at rock bottom, fitness-wise.

But it wasn't just my physical fitness that became a concern. I had read a leaflet about what to expect after heart surgery and it had clearly said that depression was a likely side effect. I gather it's the anaesthetic, so it probably affects all people post-op. I am a very positive person and just discounted any thought this would happen to me. It did though, and those around me would suffer for many months afterwards.

Looking back, the best way of dealing with the fairly regular bouts of depression would have been to confront the problem and discuss it openly with my then girlfriend, now wife, and my family. It wasn't discussed though, not until a long time after, when at times comments about my behaviour during that period came as a total shock to me. When I thought about specific instances, though, I realised I had, at times, been downright bloody awful to be around.

To tell the truth, I don't think I have ever since felt the way I used to feel before my operation either physically or mentally. It's not clear-cut, though, because the ageing process will no doubt have had an effect. All I know is that I never get the feeling of total invincibility I sometimes had when 'beating up' others on a run or cycle. Some degree of sporting recalibration was required. Even now, many years later, I long to dominate on the bike but just can't.

I am aware that some people commented – not directly to me, I might add – that after the op I had become a nicer person and less arrogant. They were right and I still feel that now (although there are occasional lapses!). I think a lot of that is down to greater maturity but also the life-changing event that open heart surgery is; it did make me take stock of my life. My quest, though, has been to minimise the change; my outlook on life and drive have helped substantially with that.

Any barriers I have come across I have dealt with and taken in my stride, whether they are finding a way to absorb the massively increased cost of life assurance or not being able to drink much alcohol due to the anticoagulant medication I have to take. When I was told never to ski again, for fear of a bad fall leading to serious blood loss, I ignored the advice. Some might say that is reckless but in my view I have been given a life through a prosthetic valve and want to live it!

Six weeks after the operation, during my follow-up consultation with the cardiologist, I casually asked what would have happened if they hadn't diagnosed my problem. He looked at me across the table with a very grave face, saying, 'You would probably have been out running one day and that would have been it.' I didn't need to ask what 'it' was.

Now, I am obviously not a doctor, but in total layman's terms and for those of you interested, my mitral valve was what is referred to as prolapsed and rather than acting as a one-way valve it was letting blood flow both ways. This had been seriously affecting the performance of the heart, which was substantially dilated – larger than it should have been – due to the extra work it had had to do. For good measure, I also had a small 'hole' in the heart, apparently caused by the blood flow from the failed valve. The surgeon told me afterwards he 'fixed that easily with a couple of stitches'.

A 30-YEAR CYCLE

With my new valve clicking away it took me ages to get back into any form of sport. To begin with a flight of stairs or slight incline made me seriously out of breath but gradually my fitness returned. I could run a lot easier than before but nowhere near what I had been used to; more like a fast jog, I guess. It quickly became clear that to get back to anything like I was before the op fitness-wise would take a lot of effort.

I kidded myself at one point that I would run the London Marathon again and entered through the ballot – luckily I wasn't successful. I actually did very little apart from skiing, and of course that was forbidden on the basis I was now on anticoagulant drugs. I still ski at least twice a year although I do take it fairly easy.

My life was to become fairly sedentary. I occasionally ran, or rather jogged, but did nothing like I had before. My weight increased and luckily due to my height – I'm well over six foot – it didn't really show. A change in the law and a more relaxed medical regime meant I did eventually learn to fly a light aircraft on a restricted licence and also flew microlights, moving on to become a flying instructor. The ironic thing being that due to my prosthetic valve and anticoagulant treatment I was forced down a route of flying aircraft that was seen by many insurers to be partaking in a dangerous sport.

So my very active life of before my operation was over. All those I talked to amongst my medical advisors just took the view that I should be glad to be alive. They told me not to worry about running marathons, skiing across the Alps and climbing snowy peaks, all things I had done in the years since packing in cycling.

The sad thing is, for quite a few years I agreed with them. They were very enjoyable years, with a new wife, second son and many fun times, but I often reflected on what might have been. I still watched cycling on the TV, even made it to Paris in 1999 to see a certain American cyclist, by what we now know was cheating, win his first Tour de France. I would periodically enjoy brief forays into the local Hampshire countryside on my beloved vintage Marin mountain bike and ponder on what I could do, but left it at that.

Although more active sports were on hold, it only took me a year to get back to skiing. My operation meant I missed out on a boys' ski trip I had organised, which had been a tour of Mont Blanc on skis. Now, this is a regular summer walking route and from what I had found out through discussions with my good friend and mountain guide, Mark, it appeared it had never been done on skis before. Anyway, following my idea, the boys did go and had a nightmare time in very bad weather. The members of the group didn't get on either, so probably a good one to have missed.

I was desperate to get skiing again after missing the ill-fated Mont Blanc trip. The following year an easier itinerary of heli-skiing was planned. I figured that would be more relaxed than slogging uphill on skis. Problem was, after very little physical exercise, how would I cope? Sitting in a helicopter wasn't going to stretch me but a long off-piste descent definitely would. One amazing thing was that many of those around me, including my wife, have no idea of the rigours of a long ski descent. I was worried, but due to my confident nature did bugger all to get fit. I did however drive up to the Midlands to the newly opened Tamworth Snowdome in order to check I could still ski! Not surprisingly, I could. And after three descents of the very short and easy slope, probably putting in no more than ten turns in all, I left, got back in the car and drove home. The following week I was standing on top of a mountain with my mate, Kev, ready to start our descent!

There were six of us in our ski party and we couldn't all fit in the helicopter, so this necessitated two 'drops'. Kev and I went in the first one with most of the group's skis and the others were to follow on the next drop. For 20 minutes or so we both stood on the small mountain summit waiting for our guide and the rest of the group, laughing about the fact it was only a year ago I had had heart surgery and about my brief training trip to Tamworth. The laughter did turn a little nervous, though, when the others took a while to arrive.

As it turned out I coped with the day well and felt amazingly good.

I was spurred on by this skiing performance. So with the improving spring weather, my new fitness regime became regular weekend jogs with our Labrador, Walter. During the week, though, I did nothing. I couldn't really do anything as I was commuting on an early train to London and working very long days. I would occasionally walk from Waterloo to the office in an attempt to get some midweek exercise but the slightest drizzle or even hint of rain and I headed straight for the Tube.

What I really didn't like about not being fit was that I couldn't get involved with the sorts of endurance events I had been used to. I also didn't like my expanding waistline and flabby appearance but accepted this on the basis that middle age had arrived. I can see now how easy it is to just enjoy life and give up serious competitive exercise, but deep down it just doesn't suit me. I like eating, drinking and everything that goes around that, but I also like to compete and enjoy being able to do active things without being left behind or aching for days afterwards.

Straight to the heart of it

One of the things I hated was people knowing about my heart valve. On boys' skiing trips it was difficult hiding it, especially from my roommates. As many would know, snoring can become a major issue when a group of blokes share the same room. In my case it was the slow click, click, click of my prosthetic valve that could be heard during the quiet of the night.

I was always keen to prove I wasn't some sort of invalid as this was sometimes the way I felt. This regularly got me thinking about things I might be able to do. Surprisingly, looking back, the cycling idea took a while to come my way.

Back in the saddle

In 2008 I decided to run the London Marathon again. What made me do this? I think it was partly because I missed having something to aim for that wasn't work-related. I also felt horribly unfit with the weight I had put on.

In the years after my heart operation I had faced many challenges. None of them revolved around sport. I had challenging jobs, worked with a team to publicly float a company, tried to buy another, set up and ran a start-up. They were all fulfilling but not in the same way to me as being successful at something that required physical endeavour.

I had taken part in the London Marathon twice before in consecutive years, 1994 and 1995, before my heart operation, and it was partly this that drove me to do it again. Could I regain my earlier fitness and run it again? This was a recurring theme that would play out with cycling a little while later. Curiosity as to how I would cope with training, plus the prospect of raising money for charity as well as the substantial challenge of running 26.2 miles gave me the motivation.

Anyway, I did it. After many months of training with my faithful Labrador, Walter, who accompanied me on all my runs, long and short, I found myself standing on the start line in Greenwich, south-east London. It was great to be back and more than a little emotional, doing

Back in the saddle

something that still felt very familiar all those years later on a fine and sunny April morning.

For some reason, though, it wasn't to be my day. I felt slow from the start and by 13 miles, just around the halfway point, I began to feel awful. This was compounded by the fact that you can clearly see the runners who are on the return leg of the course, in their final few miles as you head out in the opposite direction to Canary Wharf.

I was so fed up, but after all the hours spent training, my determination and pride wouldn't let me give in. All I could do was jog along at a very slow pace; my legs felt like rubber and nausea started to take over. If it had been like the previous two times I had taken part when Canary Wharf had been devoid of spectators and windswept, I am sure I would have packed it in. But this time around, with all the development around there in the intervening years it was full of spectators who helped create an almost party atmosphere. They, with their shouts of encouragement and the general cacophony of noise, kept me going. I was in my own world of pain but nothing was going to stop me finishing.

And I did finish, but in an appallingly bad time of 5 hours and 15 minutes – almost walking pace, 45 minutes beyond the target I had set and 90 minutes slower than my previous times. I did beat Jordan and Peter Andre, at least, but they probably had lots of distractions en route.

After the finish, I held myself together to collect my belongings and then just had to sit down, I felt faint and sick and not very well at all. The weather had been unseasonably warm and there were a few victims of this; I was determined not to be one of them. To add to my problems I couldn't get hold of my wife and my mother on my mobile. I just sat on the ground, people laughing

A 30-YEAR CYCLE

and joking around me, and waited as I gradually started to feel normal again. I often find that after exercise I go through a period of an hour or so of feeling pretty shitty. When this passes, though, I become ravenous.

I did that day. After being reunited with my family I was soon tucking into a large pizza. I must admit I had to laugh as people in the restaurant congratulated me on my London Marathon medal which I wore with pride. To them my time didn't count; finishing did. Anyone who has completed a marathon gets immediate respect from most people. I guess they should, really. As my doctor said, 'A marathon is just a little too far for the human body to cope with easily.' It is probably the biggest endurance challenge most adults get involved in, often driven by a cause and raising vast amounts for charity. Perhaps those people have the right idea and the taking part really is what it is all about.

As you may imagine, I soon resolved that the 2009 London event would be my last marathon on the basis that my performance wouldn't get any better. I would just have to do something else to quench my competitive thirst. At that stage I just didn't know what.

I did keep jogging, though, just to maintain fitness, for my annual boys' ski trip if nothing else.

A year or so later a chance comment in my local pub put bike riding back on the agenda.

'There's a cycle event at Highclere Castle in May. Why don't you guys do it?'

A simple question during a wide-ranging conversation about cars, work, sport, money and the annual ski trip, the sort of chatter that ensued every Friday night in the pub. The discussion on the cycle event was very brief but I made a mental note to check it out.

Back in the saddle

My group of drinking friends, mainly near neighbours, met every Friday to let off steam: something that probably goes on in different ways all over the UK and indeed around the world at the end of the traditional working week. Men having the opportunity to drink six or seven pints, fart, belch and then stagger home to their long-suffering wives, who would have to endure a night with the duvet floating slightly above the bed on a pungent cloud of beer fumes! The older ones in the group getting up three or four times to urinate as their internal system responded to the weekly shock of nearly a gallon of alcohol!

Some days later I did some research on Google. I found out that the cycling event was much bigger than I had imagined. It was also something I hadn't heard of before, an event called a 'sportive' with distances to be covered that ranged from a ride with kids of only 3 miles up to 127 miles for the really serious cyclist.

I circulated an email to some of my pub mates and a few of us signed up to ride the sensible-seeming distance of 45 miles. The following weekend during another alcohol-fuelled session, this time at a party in our local village hall, it was agreed we would meet early the next morning to start training for the event. It was only a month or so away!

I remember our first 'training session' well. There was a motley collection of mountain bikes sat upon by a scruffy group of guys ranging from being mildly overweight to probably clinically obese. One thing was common, though: we all had hangovers.

We set off at a fairly slow pace, just as men do when they are uncertain as to the fitness of their peers and don't want to be shown up in the first mile at any rate. The initial route was very pleasant in the cool morning

A 30-YEAR CYCLE

spring sunshine. Pete, who clearly knew the local area best, led the group and we soon found ourselves bumping and slipping over the rough terrain of farm tracks and bridleways to the west of where we lived.

Inevitably the opportunity to hit some hills came before too long. We began a long climb up on to the Wayfarers Way to the south-west of our home village of Highclere in Hampshire. To my amazement I actually felt good and fairly comfortably pedalled up the long grassy path ahead of the others. The residual fitness from my marathon running was clearly still there. It would be one of the few times in the coming years and months that I would be in that position on a hill!

When we finally reached the ridge we followed the Wayfarers Way for a while, enjoying the views of Berkshire to the north and Hampshire and Wiltshire to the south. Life back on a bike was good, especially with the camaraderie of a group. A brief shower that turned from light rain to hail and then abruptly stopped didn't spoil our enjoyment but actually made the descent more fun as we slipped and slid along our now muddy route.

Two fun-packed hours later we were back at home, all exhilarated and already talking about the next weekend's ride; the die was cast, a group called the Wayfarers Wheelers was formed and regular rides began. Over the next few weeks we met at every weekend and often midweek too. It was an amazing transformation from beer-swilling middle-aged guys to cyclists. Beer and eating still played a big part, though; after each Sunday ride we would re-group at one house or another to have a few post-race beers and a bacon butty.

Gradually, as things became more serious and the rides a lot longer, the post-ride refreshments became alcohol-free and less sociable – we were too tired!

Back in the saddle

L–R: Pete Dunmore, Matt Franklin, The Author – finishing The Magnificat 2009. The first sportive on my return to cycling.

The Highclere sportive was only the start. Within three or four short months we had gone from riding on poorly maintained and in some cases very heavy mountain bikes to all owning carbon-framed racing machines. Steve, the only Scot in our contingent, was the last to give in and buy a new bike and probably benefited from being the last; having to power his heavy bike along keeping up with us aided his fitness no end, and when he finally got on a lighter bike his performance was even more impressive.

We rode not only the local 45-mile event together but also a handful of other sportives over the next few months. Cycling came to dominate all our lives to a certain extent. As the only former cyclist in the group I was very happy to be back in the saddle and became the self-appointed organiser, coming up with new ideas on

A 30-YEAR CYCLE

what events to ride, suggesting training routes and also teaching key cycling skills like 'through and off' and the benefits of drafting other riders.

One of the most fun things I introduced to the group was the age-old club run tradition of sprinting for village signs. Before too long we were scaring fellow road users with some flat-out sprints for these signs. They became as important to us at times as a Tour de France stage win!

There were some very amusing times. Guys sprinting for the wrong signs. It's only village signs that count, not general road signage. Sometimes individuals would break away and be told by me that it was totally unacceptable; attacking two miles or more from a sign just wasn't on. The general rule was that as soon as the sign was in sight it became fair game and the two-wheeled battle could begin. It made for some nervous times as villages approached. Some were better than others at remembering where particular village signs were located and there was lots of tactical riding – just like in a real race.

As ever when blokes get together, no matter how relaxed it all starts, testosterone soon kicks in and our bike rides together often became very competitive. On occasion it would be a few miles at speed, with individual riders taking it in turns to lead the group until eventually it would all break down. This could be caused by a weaker member of the group failing to keep their place and allowing a gap to form but at other times by a mechanical problem or a puncture.

Any hill we came across was an opportunity for a mini-race, especially the longer ones, but there would always be a re-grouping at the top. Most of the time it was all conducted in good humour, but there was the occasional strop due to a bad day, a hangover or just a general lack of fitness. We had the odd bike thrown down in anger and the silent treatment with a rider preferring to suffer in their own thoughts. On a couple of occasions, we had those who just pleaded to be left behind and make their own way home. When you are having an off-day or are just plain knackered this can be the best way to deal with it rather than hanging on.

Bike riding, like many sports, can be a great leveller. In a sick sort of way – and it's very unfriendly, I know – when new riders came along they would often get a complete working over. One Sunday morning, Fran, a very fit guy we knew, turned up on his mountain bike. He powered along on the front of the group for at least the first hour, grinding away in a really big gear. As soon as we hit the hills he was history and the next two hours or so were spent trying to keep him with us, regularly waiting at the top of hills for him to catch up. In the last few miles he was totally in pieces and couldn't stop apologising for slowing us down; a broken man. This happened a few times with various guys, some fit, others less so, who had a compete nightmare, but in all cases the general camaraderie came through and we always finished the ride together.

From my teenage years I had been taught on club runs that the group should stick together, in effect riding at the pace of the slowest rider. I often found myself to be the 'policeman' of this particular rule of riding etiquette, especially when the group's temptation to have a 'burn-up' in the last few miles became overwhelming, as it often did.

There were times, though, when things did just fall apart. On one ride during a wet Sunday in January just about everyone in the group suffered at least one

A 30-YEAR CYCLE

puncture. In fact we completely ran out of spare inner tubes, even those who very sensibly carried two. In the end, I was the only one to make it all the way home under my own steam. We lost Mark early on to a double wheel puncture, forcing him to take sanctuary at his sister's house, Pete and Steve had to call for a lift and Stuart rode his tyre flat! When it finally disintegrated he called for a taxi. Luckily we only experienced this sort of puncture-fest once and that was enough; the day in question is still talked about now.

I had similar experiences many years before. One of our club runs used to go to a place called Consall Forge in the Staffordshire Peak District, where there was a rustic pub that made an ideal lunch stop. It was normally the venue for the club's Christmas lunch. The problem was that getting to the pub involved some riding on rough country tracks, not roads. Punctures were inevitable but were also the least of our problems. The final track to the pub led to a bridge across a small stream. This bridge was made of two planks that unfortunately had a gap of about a tyre's width between them. As you can imagine it was almost inevitable that one of the guys would place his front wheel neatly between the planks. One did. His nickname was 'the Ayatollah'. I turned a corner to see him still on his bike but with the front wheel jammed up to the forks in the gap. Fortunately no real damage had been done but he was quite shaken and unusually quiet for the rest of the day!

The other funny thing on that particular trip was the requirement after lunch to ride down the flight of steps in front of the pub. This required a lot of skill and often the rider would end up going over the bars while trying to brake and balance their way down the steps.

I made it unscathed to the pub but my problems

started after we left. I punctured twice before we made the metalled road again. It was wet and muddy and as I was using tubular tyres the replacements wouldn't stick properly. They kept rolling around the rim and I ended up riding on the tyre sidewall. I had no option but to keep stopping to sort the problem out and after a while my chums got fed up and left me. How I managed to get home that day, a ride of over 30 miles, without another puncture, I will never know!

Club members regularly carried out pranks on one another. Some of the so-called fun on club runs was quite brutal on the recipients. There were things called 'mangelwurzels'; I know it sounds like a made-up word but I have recently discovered a mangelwurzel is a root vegetable used mostly for feeding livestock. Some may well have been mangelwurzels but they were mainly either turnips or swedes sometimes left in piles by local farmers at the side of country roads. This is how they were deployed: without the rest of the group knowing, someone would pick up a so-called mangelwurzel from the side of the road and then from the back they would 'bowl' it like a ten-pin bowling ball forwards through the group, shouting the brief warning 'Mangelwurzel!' at the same time. It would cause panic and total chaos in the group as riders sought to avoid the mangelwurzel bouncing around in the road. Occasionally some guys might fall off through colliding with one another and sometimes the mangelwurzel would just hit riders and give them a real fright. Great fun at the time but it all seems totally reckless now and more than a little unfair on your riding colleagues. It did create some laughs though. Luckily I don't remember anyone ever getting seriously hurt or bikes getting damaged.

Setting the objective – relive my youth!

My dream to complete a stage of the Tour de France had ended on the lower slopes of the Tourmalet. For the first time ever, I had failed to finish something I had set out to do. Everyone who knew me was surprised. They asked questions, probably passed judgement, but most, I am sure, didn't really care. Initially I felt I couldn't face anyone, but I would have to at some stage. When asked how I had got on in the Étape du Tour, I just said, 'It was the hardest thing I have ever done.' Actually, it wasn't, but at least it closed the conversation down.

Having got back into cycling, the passion of my youth, I certainly didn't want to give it up now I was in my late forties. Although publicly I kept quiet and accepted the regular teasing of my Étape teammates and others, after my Étape failure, I had thought about and decided what I could do next on my bike.

I have already talked about my visit to my cardiologist to get checked out before any serious commitments to racing were made. My wife and parents quite rightly thought I was mad to push myself any more. I needed some medical reassurance.

I lay bare-chested on the hospital bed in a dimly lit room. I had been through this routine many times before during echocardiograms. But this time I was more

Setting the objective – relive my youth!

worried; I was concerned my episode in the Pyrenees might have done some serious damage that would destroy any plans I might have.

'Sniff.'

I did.

'Thanks,' said the nurse.

'Never been asked to do that before; is there a problem?' I asked.

'No, no. There is just an artery that collapses when you sniff and I hadn't been able to locate it; now I have,' she said.

I remained worried as to the potential significance of this but assumed I would learn more when I saw the cardiologist later.

When I finally did see him, he greeted me in his normal friendly way and I immediately assumed all was well. Luckily, it was OK and, like his response to my London Marathon performance, he didn't really comment on my Étape failure. It was as if he was thinking, *Why do you expect anything else? You have got a prosthetic heart valve, after all*.

He made a comment:

'What you have to remember is that the mitral valve in a normal person will actually dilate and increase in size to allow more blood to flow. Yours is fixed.'

'It's like my engine is governed,' I said.

'Correct.'

Hmm, I thought, that doesn't sound great, but at least all is well.

With a clean bill of health I was able to firm up on my plan, one that required rolling back the years to replicate a performance of my youth. The inner motivation for this was to prove – more to myself than to anyone else – that I could still really perform on a bike despite my heart

A 30-YEAR CYCLE

valve. I had accepted that the cols of the Pyrenees wouldn't be my focus, but the flatter roads of the UK would.

Sometime in 1981, around June or July, I rode in a 25-mile time trial. This was unusual for me as my main interest and focus at the time had always been road racing. Anyway, my dad always said I was better at time trialling. He was right! I was in the prize money for the event in a time of 59:58. Not exceptional even by the standards of the day and positively slow in the 21st century but a good time nevertheless, and all done on a normal road bike with none of the aerodynamic frills or skinsuits that are now the norm. Sub-hour rides for 25 miles are still a benchmark for all cyclists, but little could I have imagined then that this would become a personal target 30 years later.

My 'first' time trialling career had been a fairly limited one; I probably only rode a handful of events, a mixture

Going under the hour in a 25-mile time trial 1981.

Setting the objective – relive my youth!

of 5-, 10- and mainly 25-mile tests. All my times were written down in my training diaries which had long since disappeared, but some times I had very clearly etched in my memory:

Ten miles: 23:42.

Twenty-five miles: 1:00:40 – wow, that was close! I had also managed the same distance in 1:01:23 using a junior gear of 86.4 inches, which I was particularly proud of in view of the high cadence that had been required.

There was no chance of replicating that last performance – I just can't pedal that fast any longer! But it was mainly the 59:58, under the 'magic' hour, that stuck in my memory and it became my objective: to ride the same course or, at the very least, a 25-mile event in the same time or faster, before I was too old or some other impediment came my way.

The first thing I had to check was that the course actually still existed. Many of the courses I had competed on in the Midlands had long since become defunct. They were victims of increased traffic making them too dangerous for cycling, changes to road layout, new motorways cutting through them and even traffic lights that made racing on them impossible.

Luckily for me, the course concerned, code-named K16/25 by Cycling Time Trials, the governing body for the sport in the UK, still existed. It had changed a bit, especially at the turn, but fundamentally it was the same course.

I remembered that the last time I had ridden on this stretch of road. The event had been held on a Saturday afternoon. No chance of that now, with traffic the way it is – all events there have to be held on a Sunday with the last rider finished by 9 am. So I was resigned to an early

A 30-YEAR CYCLE

start, usually around 7 am. Luckily my mum still lived locally, so a good night's sleep was still possible.

The first time I thought I was on track for my target was when I recorded a 25:38 in a 10-mile time trial one Saturday. Nothing exciting in that, but it was a time well within the standard veteran's target for my age group over that distance – I was finally getting competitive! To put my performance into context, however, the event was won by Team Sky rider Alex Dowsett in 18:36 with another time trialling specialist, Michael Hutchings, second in 19:03.

Regardless of being so far off the pace, it was good enough for me. The next day I decided to show all my Wayfarers Wheelers colleagues who was boss! I should have known from my years of experience that it was best not to show off, especially when you were pedalling with a disadvantage.

I forced the pace and we covered the first 15 miles or so at over 18 mph. Very fast for us middle-aged, mainly weekend bike riders. I felt great, so great I outsprinted my naturally fit brother-in-law, Marwood, for an uphill village sign. It took me nearly two miles to recover because the pace was well over 20 mph.

Then another opportunity to shine came along; I forced the pace up a small hill. The group fractured and then at the top a small dog ran out and I narrowly missed it. The others thought I had been spooked by this and that was why I suddenly slowed down. Not so; I was in real difficulty.

Due to my heart condition, I can suffer from something called atrial fibrillation where the heart beats very fast – well over 200 beats per minute. My cardiologist has always warned me about this happening and if it does to stop, sit down and rest until normality is

Setting the objective – relive my youth!

restored. Did I heed his advice? No, I tried to carry on at a slower pace, not wanting to get left totally behind.

For the rest of the ride I was in all kinds of trouble. My heart did come down from over 200 bpm to around 150 bpm but no matter how easily I pedalled along it wouldn't slow down any further. I just couldn't keep up, and after the others waited for me a couple of times only for me to be dropped again, they gave up and left me. My brother-in-law even hung back and tried to pace me back to the group, but it was to no avail; I just couldn't go at speed. I was finished.

In fact I was just happy to ride along slowly; my tail was firmly between my legs. I had paid dearly for my stupidity in forcing the pace and resolved not to do it again.

Luckily, I knew where we planned to stop for coffee in Hungerford and wobbled up to park in front of the café five minutes or so after the others. By this time they were relaxing over drinks and cake. My heart still racing, I ordered what I wanted and sat quietly, not really part of all the banter. Instead of my usual coffee I had ordered tea, not wanting to give my heart another boost with excessive caffeine.

By the time we left the café I did feel normal again and luckily it was an easy 15 miles or so home, although I got dropped again. I was wasted and just rode home slowly on my own. So much for teaching them who was boss!

It had felt good, though, to put the others under pressure, and to this day, or at least until they read this book, they have no idea why I started so strongly and then blew up so spectacularly. No, guys, it wasn't the dog!

The onset of atrial fibrillation has only happened to

A 30-YEAR CYCLE

me a couple of times, and only when I have really pushed it. I know now when it might come on; my heart slows down a bit and then *whoosh*, it's all of a sudden beating at over 200! Now if it does happen I do stop. Atrial fibrillation can carry a risk of a stroke, which I certainly don't want, and I understand the heart can get stuck beating at that level. The treatment then is a procedure in hospital to stop the heart and start it again. Don't fancy that.

Although I was committed to training and racing towards my sub-hour objective I continued to ride with my mates on their long Sunday rides. I also still wanted to ride a bike for fun. After suffering and giving up the Tourmalet in the previous year's Étape I organised a couple of easier trips the following year, one to Antibes in the south of France, the other to take in some of the mountain stages of the Tour de France and the finish in Paris.

The trip to Antibes included our wives, who got to spend three days by the pool while we headed inland into the mountains. Great training; after negotiating an exit from the busy roads of Antibes, half the distance of the rides would be uphill and the return half mainly downhill. It was nice also to be in good weather.

The daily routine was punishing, though. Our rides always followed a good night out in one of the local restaurants where we certainly didn't hang back on the food or wine. Riding fast along the coastal strip the next morning towards Nice was an excellent hangover cure, though, and of course once the route turned uphill, the sweat and pain of the seemingly incessant climb soon put paid to the effects of the excesses of the night before.

One thing that impressed us was the large groups of French riders we came across, always in a neat

Setting the objective – relive my youth!

formation and immaculately turned out in matching club kit. We in our multi-coloured kit of various types felt like tramps by comparison. I have never seen anything that impressive on British roads. But there again, we certainly gave them a run for their money when they tried to pass us. One morning three of us sat on the front of the group of French guys we had joined, steadily tapping away on the pedals as we climbed away from the coast. No one from the French group came through to take a turn at the front. It was only when one of our small group of three dropped back and we had to wait for him to catch up again that our British-dominated fun came to an end.

My lasting memory of the trip was the descents back to Antibes at the end of each ride. We were nearly always in excess of the speed limit and often overtaking cars. Beers and a sandwich lunch around the pool back at the hotel beckoned; after a tough ride we couldn't wait to get back to relax and recover for the next day, and of course a big night out.

The thing about cycling around the Côte d'Azur is that the rides entail spending at least three quarters of the time going uphill and then the other quarter coming back down. There is no real in-between unless you fancy a ride along the busy coastal strip. It's true that, this being France, the car drivers are far more accommodating to cyclists and the French equivalent of the UK's 'white van man' doesn't seem to exist, so even in traffic it is more pleasant, but I prefer the quieter, very picturesque albeit hilly roads that head inland.

The trip to follow the last four stages of the Tour de France, as such trips often are, was sadly more about spectating than riding a bike.

We stayed in the Alpine village of La Grave, which

was well located for two of the major mountain finishes and even the penultimate day's TT in Grenoble.

The trip got off to an interesting start. Rather than pay the rather large hire fee for a minibus, I did a deal with a friend who ran a local boys' football team to borrow his. We really appreciated the loan of the bus, especially as it was at a very competitive price, but my heart sank as I drove away after picking it up and pulled down the sun visor to see '*This vehicle has been restricted to a maximum speed of 100km per hour*'. This would have a big impact on the trip.

Our journey to La Grave began at 5.30 am on Wednesday 20th July and ended as we pulled into the attractive La Meije campsite 16 hours later. We stopped only twice for food, a pee and fuel, otherwise it was foot flat to the floor. At times we managed to get 120kph out of the minibus, but only when coasting downhill and it actually felt very unstable at that speed. You could feel the anxiety from all the guys, concerned about what would happen if, say, a tyre burst. I don't think it would have taken that much for whoever was driving to lose control.

In order to maximise speed, one other stunt for whoever was driving the bus was to sit really close drafting behind a lorry and then pop out from behind and overtake. It became quite fun to race lorries in this way and apart from eating, drinking, reading a book or listening to music, this lorry drafting was the only entertainment on our long journey.

When we arrived very late in La Grave, it being a small Alpine village, almost everything was closed. After putting the tents up in the dark it was off to a bar to grab a pizza and some beers. This was followed by a miserable night in the freezing cold. Hard to believe it

Setting the objective – relive my youth!

was mid-July. We heard that it had snowed on top of the Galibier that day, which was to be our objective for the next morning and the finish of stage 18 of the Tour.

The next day was overcast but slightly warmer and after a quick, very impromptu breakfast of jam and croissants we got ready and set off to climb the Col du Lautaret with the aim of pushing on from there and riding to the top of the Galibier. This was fairly easy going and the weather gradually improved as we neared the col. The sheer number of people riding their bikes reminded me of the Étape but there were also more vehicles parked and lots of pedestrians ambling onto the course.

On reaching the col, we were told by some very aggressive gendarmes that the route to the Galibier was closed to all vehicles, including bikes. It was only 10 am and the Tour wasn't due to arrive until nearly 4 pm! I had diligently planned our day and checked all the planned road closures. The road from the Col du Lautaret to the Galibier wasn't meant to close until 1 pm. I went to remonstrate with a gendarme but thought better of it when one of his colleagues literally pushed a Belgian cyclist and his bike back from the road block. Apparently they were concerned about safety and too many people being on the twisting road up to the summit.

None of us was carrying food and the weather was cool and windy with some threatening clouds overhead, so a quick decision was made to descend to Serre Chevalier. 'Don't worry,' I said to the group, 'we can have lunch there and climb back up to the Lautaret to watch the race.' Little did I know the gendarmerie would intervene again!

After a fantastic descent, spoiled only by having to avoid official vehicles speeding in the opposite direction,

A 30-YEAR CYCLE

we met some more gendarmes at the roadside. To our total dismay we were told they would be closing the road in 30 minutes. Bang went our lunch in Serre Chevalier. As you may imagine, we had become fragmented during the descent, bearing in mind not everyone wanted to plummet down the twisting road at 40 mph plus, like me and Simon. It took a while to regroup, especially waiting for the more cautious descenders.

There was nothing more to do than climb back up the col and find a position where we would get a good view. Ideas abounded and one was to stop off at a roadside restaurant for lunch. We quickly found this wouldn't be possible. They were either (amazingly) closed or (not so amazingly) full!

In the end we found a perfect place, just opposite a large Belgian group cooking and selling their own burgers and offering cold beers too. Music was blaring away: a mix of eighties hits and almost every four or five songs Joe Dassin's cheerful little ditty, 'Champs Élysées'. This would become the signature tune for the trip – we heard it on the slopes of Alpe D'Huez, down in Grenoble and inevitably in Paris too. Such a fitting tune bearing in mind the whole Tour is ultimately focused on reaching the famous boulevard to celebrate the eventual winner.

The long wait for the Tour to pass began, four hours to be exact. The weather was mixed, only the odd rain shower and then bursts of brilliant sunshine, but there was a stiff wind that kept us cool. Without the Belgian burgers and our cheerful banter it would have been unbearable. One of the things to pass the time was the very obvious need of various gathered spectators to tend to a call of nature. They all disappeared behind the same bushes on the steep mountainside.

It wasn't long before one of our group needed to go.

Setting the objective – relive my youth!

Steve announced he needed a crap. Off he headed to a round of applause from the by now large audience. I think most of the spectators decided to wait until later.

As late afternoon approached, the so-called Tour 'caravan' passed along the road with all of the race sponsors' vehicles, some, as usual, throwing freebies to the spectators. Just like many others we behaved like little children, scrambling to collect whatever mementos were being thrown at us. After this, expectations grew as the leading riders were spotted climbing up the road below us. They soon passed; the Schleck brothers, eventual Tour winner Cadel Evans and other strong climbers, all riding at an impressive pace. Some stragglers soon followed and then there was a long wait for the main group going at a much steadier speed and a chance to take some great photographs.

After the excitement of the Tour passing us, we mounted our bikes to ride back up to the Col du Lautaret. This was followed by an interesting descent back to La Grave. Interesting only because it involved weaving in and out between vehicles and pedestrians. How we made it back without mishap I will never know.

Rhys, who was in our group, sadly has a degenerative eye condition. He explains that his sight is like viewing the world through a couple of toilet roll tubes. During daylight that can be dangerous enough but he amazingly manages to ride in a group without any real peripheral vision. Problem is, when it goes dark, he can't see at all. At night on the campsite we would guide him to and from the tent. During the day all would be well, although we hadn't thought about the regular road tunnels you come across while cycling in the Alps. One minute bright sunshine, the next almost pitch black. The fact that Rhys managed to navigate through dark tunnels at speeds

A 30-YEAR CYCLE

Fun at the Tour de France. L–R: The Author, Simon Holland, Rhys Phillip, Peter Dumore, Adam Syme, Steve Suttie and Mark Letsome.

well over 30 mph is a triumph for his determination. All he said he needed was a light on the bike in front and he claimed he would be OK following that. In the end there wasn't a single incident due to his failing eyesight.

We had a great second day riding the climb up to Alpe d'Huez about three or four hours before the Tour. With all the spectators there and by that time some of them very drunk, it was a wonderful experience. Our whole group of six guys split up as we each rode at our own pace, counting off the hairpins. Our efforts were rewarded by a very good and expensive meal in a

Setting the objective – relive my youth!

restaurant in Alpe d'Huez village, allowing us to kill time before the Tour arrived. We saw Pierre Roland arrive first and then hung around to see Mark Cavendish lead the Grupetto in – who should have all been eliminated on time that day, but I guess there is safety in numbers and the organisers are hardly likely to eliminate half the field!

Our escape from Alpe d'Huez felt exactly like that. The whole village was gridlocked. I really fancied the descent back the way we had climbed but after our experience the previous day on Lautaret we all agreed the traffic and pedestrians would spoil the experience. After a bit of cyclo-cross riding to get away from the throngs of spectators we made our way towards the Col de Sarenne. Initially it was a fast descent spoiled only by wheel-sized drainage channels across the narrow road. I skidded to a halt at one, figuring that hitting it at speed could mean a rapid journey over the bars.

A slow grind up to the col itself was followed by an exhilarating descent and probably the most technical I have ever done, twisting and turning back to the main road to return to La Grave. This in itself was a long pull and our lights were required for the last couple of hours. We finally pulled into La Grave at 9 pm – a long day of over 12 hours and a bit like the Étape really.

We found the best restaurant in the village and piled in, still in our sweaty cycling kit.

'What's foie gras?' asked Mark as we ordered it as a starter.

'Your chance to find out,' said Adam.

Rhys then suggested we have a bottle of Sauterne to accompany it. The rest was and still is a blur. How we made it back to the pitch black campsite, who knows?

Sadly, the rest of the trip was spent in the minibus rather than riding our bikes, as we had to cover the long

A 30-YEAR CYCLE

distance to Paris for the Tour finish. Our long and uncomfortable drive was soon forgotten, though, as the following day we watched the exciting race finale on the Champs-Élysées and Mark Cavendish sprint to yet another stage win. The governed engine of the minibus led to our own 'race' on the journey home – against the clock and the last evening departure through the Chunnel. We missed it!

I love cycling in France and even during our annual family summer holidays in the Alps I have been keen to stick to my training plan. Early one evening, after a morning's climbing with my kids and then a leisurely lunch by the pool, I decided to head out for a couple of hours before dinner. The weather was fine, warm and sunny but there were threatening clouds on the horizon as I pedalled furiously up the Col des Montets.

After reaching the summit of the col, my route followed one of my favourite descents down through Vallorcine and to the Swiss border. Feeling good and with the weather still fine I carried on over the border, through the delightful Swiss village of Trient and up to the top of the Col de la Forclaz. As I neared the top of Forclaz light rain began to fall. I had always planned to turn around and head for home there, and due to the rain I decided to give a coffee at the café a miss.

I had been looking forward to descending Forclaz at speed but this wasn't to be. In less than a couple of minutes the rain was pouring down and I could hear the sound of distant thunder. The road became a raging torrent and day turned to night; I was soon soaking wet. I had a waterproof with me but it was ineffective in the rain. It was, however, brilliant white; just as well, I thought, as I had no lights and felt very exposed.

Setting the objective – relive my youth!

I did consider calling my wife to come and get me but then found there was no mobile signal, so I decided to press on at a pretty slow pace in view of the conditions. Luckily I made it back to the border without mishap and began my ascent of the Col des Montets, but I was clearly heading into the eye of the storm. The rain bounced off the road and my front wheel cut a wake as I ploughed through the water cascading down the road.

Just when I was a mile or so from the summit the lightning began. Fuck, I thought, just my luck to get hit by a lightning strike. The growing darkness was frequently lit up by the lightning, illuminating the mountains around me. It became very frightening and eerily quiet; the flow of cars seemed to have stopped; there was no one but me battling along the road.

After what seemed an eternity, I reached the summit unscathed but soaked to the skin. I was then able to freewheel back down towards Argentière. Just as I came around the last hairpin, not in my usual style but cautiously as though expecting to slide off, a pair of headlights fixed me in their view. It was my wife. Worried, she had set out to effect a rescue.

Due to the nature of the road it was difficult for her to turn around and I wasn't planning on stopping so I carried on to our chalet. By the time she arrived back I was stripped off and in the shower, gradually warming up my aching limbs.

I don't normally go out in the rain; I nearly always wimp out and head straight for the comfort of the turbo in the garage. It had been an exhilarating ride but fear had kicked in, especially when the lightning had started. I knew full well the risks and why being in the mountains in a thunderstorm is not sensible. I resolved to watch the weather more closely in the future.

A 30-YEAR CYCLE

These trips, although thoroughly enjoyable and good for base miles, were not going to help me with my plan to replicate my 1981 time trial performance. Most of my time was focused on this: the 'objective', as it became known. But travels like these are what makes cycling the fun it is. Enjoying days out with mates or just on your own in wonderful terrain.

Racing again

The cycling I was doing with my usual group of mates – the sportives, even the Étape, not to mention the occasional French trips – was great, but what I really yearned for was to race. People often talk about football being the 'beautiful game'; well, I think cycle racing, and I am talking about road racing in particular here, is truly the beautiful sport. What is a more impressive sight than a fast-riding group of suntanned cyclists in a cacophony of team colours moving like an organised shoal of fish, set against an awesome Alpine landscape?

OK, real grass roots racing isn't like that, it's often cold and wet and the scenery not so impressive. We can all dream, though!

I knew that road racing was sadly well out of reach for someone with my level of fitness and in view of my heart issues I was not able to cope with rapid changes of pace. My ability to climb had also not improved with passing age.

Perhaps because I was so shit at climbing hills I have always been a good descender on a bike. I remember with dread a junior road race in the early eighties during which we had to climb a nasty ascent on the Stiperstones in Shropshire a few times. For every lap, I had taken the advice of my coach to be at the front of the bunch; by the time we were halfway up the climb I had been dropped and would be wallowing around trying to make

Birches Valley Road Race, 1981.

the summit. After some crazy descending I did manage to get back to the bunch on each lap and even finish in the main group.

Although I am still crap at climbing, I seem to have held on to my natural talent for fast descending. Either that, or perhaps I just have a very high fear threshold or a lack of imagination regarding what might happen if I come off.

My wife sees it as a complete lack of any regard for her, my sons and the rest of my family. She's not the only one! My doctor has also commented on my fast descents, worrying about the injuries I could sustain if I came off, which would only be compounded by the anti-coagulant drugs I am on due to my prosthetic heart valve.

Since the early eighties, my talent for many things on a bike has disappeared, climbing in particular (whatever talent I might have had for that in the first place), but when it comes to riding at speed downhill, luckily I am in my comfort zone. I just feel at home on the bike and in total control.

There are a few hills near where I live that can be great for fast descending but they are short, full of inherent dangers, often narrow, twisting and prone to animals crossing. I think the maximum speed I have clocked in this country is 47 mph. I have had some near misses: deer (one of them a stag!), rabbits, pheasants, even squirrels; any one of those in the front wheel and it would be a trip to A&E or more.

Of course the best place to practise and enjoy the craft of high-speed descending is the Alps. Here you get long, open descents, not always that steep but sustained, with good road surfaces and with little traffic.

I have had the pleasure of quite a few Alpine descents.

A 30-YEAR CYCLE

On one in particular, coming down from the Col de la Forclaz into the Swiss town of Martigny, I once managed to hit 103.4 kph. That's nearly 65 mph. It was only very briefly and I really had to work at it.

If it wasn't for the hairpin bends on these roads I think I would be up for a land speed record, such is my determination and (limited) ability or perhaps stupidity. I love the feeling of building up the speed and tucking lower and lower on the bike, whooshing past speed signs at more than twice their indicated speed and sometimes overtaking cars, their bewildered occupants looking on.

The problem is you get very cold riding at high speed on a bike, even on a warm summer day, and the concentration required is immense. Also, every time I let my mind wander to what might happen if I puncture or meet some form of hazard, I sit up and all my good work building up speed is lost. Often I don't set out to ride as fast as possible; it just happens – I hit 45 mph or so and just keep going.

Sadly, there has been limited opportunity to use my fast descending skills and the chance certainly doesn't arise in road races.

What I could do, though, was time trialling. All that required was an initial effort to get up to speed and then holding it there in a steady state. No massive fluctuations in speed from attacks or risk of crashes from riding in close proximity. You would ride your own race, all alone against the clock and the elements, especially the wind. Not a race that would often be dictated by others.

My first time trial for 20-odd years was a 25-mile local club event organised by Newbury Road Club. I also persuaded two of my mates to join me: my neighbour, Steve, and brother-in-law, Marwood. They had no idea of what they were getting into and to be honest neither did I. I clocked 1 hour and 21 minutes and was totally embarrassed – the first of many humiliations in my second cycling 'career'. Steve beat me convincingly, going over 10 minutes faster. Poor Marwood was well adrift but only because of a puncture and even then he only lost a few minutes compared to my time. To put it into context, the winner recorded a time of around 58 minutes.

Despite the humiliation, I was hooked and the following week I was stupid enough to have a go at a much shorter and, I thought, easier 10-mile event. I think it was easier in a way – the pain only lasted just under half an hour! On this second occasion I persuaded my then 16-year-old son, Albert, to have a go too. Now all fathers will know being beaten by your kids is a seminal moment and you have guessed it: mine came then. Albert beat me by over a minute. I was really pissed off, especially as he seized on this defeat like most teenagers would and took every opportunity to remind me of this and my other apparent inadequacies as a father. I would get my own back ... in time.

Albert has only beaten me once more in a time trial and also once on what became our annual ride between Chamonix and Verbier. We often holidayed in the summer in Chamonix and I cooked up a plan to ride over to Verbier, taking the final climb the Tour de France followed. The first time we did the ride, Albert had to give up on the tough climb up to Verbier. A lack of food, the inexperience of youth and the lure of my wife coming alongside him in the car made him climb off his bike and retire, in a foul teenage mood.

The following year, it would be different; for reasons I don't really understand, apart from the fact that I had ridden every day and he was still fresh, the next time we

A 30-YEAR CYCLE

climbed to Verbier he left me completely behind. I wobbled in a good ten minutes behind him and yet again was subject to some, I felt, cruel barracking. Lesson here was 'don't race your kids'. Did I learn that day? No, it was two-all and I would wait for the next time.

And so to the next year; the annual trip finally came around again. I was fitter and attuned to Albert's natural youthful fitness. He was very confident, as you might imagine. I didn't ride the day before, as I had the previous year, and prepared myself for a hard ride, assuming a year on he would be even stronger. I decided to test his strength on one of the early climbs of the route, the Col de la Forclaz. I forced the pace and, as expected, he kept up then even passed me. I stuck with him and then forced the pace again. He kept with me. By this time I knew I had to commit and put my head down to enter my own world of suffering. Luckily for me, he faltered and before long I was 100 metres ahead. I kept going and reached the summit of the Col a good five minutes before him.

When we finally reached the last climb to Verbier I kept a steady pace and just rode away from Albert. The tables were turned. He came up to the finish 15 minutes adrift, bare-chested due to the heat and scowling. Was it worth it? Not really, it put him into a bad mood that lasted for a couple of days.

However, I was on a roll and a few days later we had a swimming 'race' at the nearby Lac de Passy. Not a short one, but over 1 kilometre. We were neck and neck for most of the course but at the end I managed to pull out the stops to beat him. My finish, though, was far from victorious. Upon making shallower water I tried to stand and walk up the shore but found myself in a kind of rubber-legged stagger, probably to the great amusement of the French sunbathers on the beach. Albert suggested we swim back, keen to have another chance to beat me.

'I'm walking,' I said.

Back at home, I really got stuck into time trialling and slowly, but far from surely, my times started to improve. Sometimes I would put in a good ride only to receive a major dent in confidence on the next outing with an awful time, for no apparent reason.

I did have another couple of goes at road racing with events run by the League of Veteran Road Cyclists. The organisation encourages veterans over 40 years old to compete and their website clearly states, '*At first you may be more comfortable competing in an older age category.*' I stupidly thought this was ridiculous and entered a race in my own 45–50 age group. You can only imagine my total humiliation when I was dropped on the first lap, not only by this group but, after falling back again and again, eventually by the group containing 80-year-olds too. I finished that first race riding with a strong guy who looked as old as my dad and he still managed to outsprint me for the line.

The following season my next two road races were no better. In the first one that year, I was dropped in lap one as the speed went from 15 mph to nearly 30 mph in a matter of seconds.

'Fucking hell, Chris,' said Simon as he came past me in a state of distress at the sudden turn of speed. He kept with it but soon succumbed, like me, to being dropped, although he finished the race. I just took my number off and gently pedalled back to the car.

The third and what turned out to be my final road race (at least at the time of writing this book!) was even

A 30-YEAR CYCLE

more of a disaster. I felt comfortable on the first lap, positioned at the front of the bunch even on a gradual climb. But as the race turned a corner and immediately hit a steeper section, yet again I slipped through and quickly out of the back of the bunch, never to regain contact.

I did come to within 10 metres of re-joining the race after I descended the hill like a demon but just didn't have the extra strength required to close the gap. Gone were the days when as a junior I would be dropped on hills regularly but easily return to the bunch on the descent or even by powering along on the flat. Oh, the pleasures of youth!

Back to time trialling: in my normal enthusiastic way, I persuaded Simon and brother-in-law Marwood to take part in a three-up team time trial. We turned up at the start to have the piss really taken out of us by the timekeepers.

'Where are your disc wheels?' said one.

'You look like cycle tourists,' said another.

And finally, 'The club run left at 10 am.'

Little did they know that Marwood had only made a last-minute decision to remove his mudguards as we had left the car. God only knows what they would have made of those!

Anyway, we had the last laugh, winning first prize in the veterans' race and a very nice bottle of red wine each. We agreed, at my instigation, to keep quiet about the fact that both of the other veterans' teams entered into the event had failed to start. I really don't think a time of 1:08 would normally be a winning time for a three-up 25-mile time trial.

I was by far the weakest link in that team, struggling to keep in formation with the others and not really pulling my weight on the front. My breathing was laboured and

Racing again

I thought my heart would burst out of my chest. At that time, I never thought I would go any faster. After all, with three of us sharing the work it surely should have been much easier.

Looking back, all my time trials in the first couple of years after returning to the sport were very disappointing. I often toyed with the idea of giving up, especially because I was so often totally humiliated even though I trained hard and would push myself as hard as I could.

I was beaten by kids, old men, old women and certainly everyone in my age group. Even so, I kept on bouncing back. I knew that although I was competing against all these people, the real test was against the clock. I just focused on that, gradually reducing my personal bests. I would like to say it was a straightforward progression, but it's just not like that. One weekend I would have a great ride, improve by a few seconds, or even over a minute in the early days, only to be knocked back the next time with an awful performance.

I would sometimes put my poor performances down to weather, strong winds especially wreaking havoc with my times. In the end, though, some of my best performances were in far from perfect conditions.

There is a term in time trialling that refers to so-called perfect conditions: a 'float' day or evening, usually midsummer. This is where the winds are light or nonexistent, it's warm and there is a high-pressure weather system so the air's density and therefore resistance to a cyclist cutting through it is low. As you can imagine, these don't come around too often in the UK!

My problem with 'float' days is purely a psychological one; I get so nervous, the pressure to perform so great that I usually have a crap ride. On one such occasion, I was feeling good and pulled up at the start after a well-planned warm-up. The club mates congregating there added to the pressure; all they said was, 'On for a PB tonight, Chris?' And that was it; my ride was fated. I sprinted away from the start, ended up going way too hard on the outward leg and struggled over the last couple of miles, only to record a mediocre time nowhere near my best.

Sometimes it's that often unfathomable thing called 'form' that is either there or not. There are times when I turn up, feel great, warm up and everything clicks and then when I start all this ebbs away. Other times I feel shit, sometimes almost ill, and then I will deliver a great time, for me anyway. I never know.

I also tried other forms of cycling. My younger son started riding at the local Reading Track League. Now, this took me back. I had really enjoyed track racing as a youth, sometimes competing up to three times a week at the local tracks at Wolverhampton, Halesowen and Birmingham. At Reading I was relegated to being a spectator at the track side, but watching the senior events really whetted my appetite. There was also a lot of cajoling from some of the dads who were competing in the adult league.

So what did I do? I bought a track bike on eBay and decided I would have a go. First, though, I had to get accredited to ride. This meant going along to training sessions. It all seemed pretty serious. The first problem I had was the fact that it didn't really fit in with my training regime. I would train as normal in the morning and by evening time, after a day's work too, I would not really be feeling up to a hard session on the track controlled by someone else and with nowhere for me to hide.

The big shock for me was the initial warm-up session, behind a derny (which is a small pedal-powered motorbike used specifically for pacing track events). It would start at a leisurely 15 mph with the riders strung out behind and then gradually build to a speed in the high 20s. I don't actually know exactly how fast as I never lasted that long and certainly not until the end of the warm-up session.

I soon realised that I wasn't going to be fast enough to cut it on the track. This perplexed me a fair bit. I could cruise at nearly 25 mph on my own in time trials but couldn't keep up even with the benefit of a slipstream behind the derny. The main reason for this was the lower fixed wheel gear used on the track. Try as I might, I just wasn't able to turn the pedals as fast as I needed to in order to travel at the required speed.

I did have some fun in the training events, riding in keirins, elimination races and sprints, but just couldn't get going due to the high cadence required. What I enjoyed most was the elimination race, often called the 'Devil'. This is where on every lap one or more of the riders who are last across the finish line are eliminated until there are just three or four riders left. They then sprint it out over one final lap for first place.

This took me back to my youth. It was always great sport to sit at the back of the group and then sprint past your fellow competitors just before the line. It works for a while and then someone does it to you or you get blocked in. The only enjoyment I got out of those evenings was the Devil and even then I would only last a handful of laps.

In the end I decided not to pursue track riding, apart from a few recreational sessions at the Calshot indoor track near Southampton. This was a whole new ball game; only 146 metres round and with banking at 46 degrees either end, it looked like the wall of death.

A 30-YEAR CYCLE

Sessions there were fun but often freezing cold – the track is in an old aircraft hangar which is unheated. Not nice. It's amazing how sometimes it can feel colder inside than out. It is OK when you are riding, but between sessions those in the know congregate around a small electric heater.

To me track racing is probably the purest form of riding a bike. The equipment is simple; no gears, no brakes and a bike stripped of any other components. You can feel completely connected with the bike through the fixed wheel not allowing you to stop pedalling.

I did ride in one track event in the end, which was for charity. Basically, a number of property industry teams came together to race. There were four events: a sprint, an elimination race, a points race and a one-lap time trial. Some of the guys there were clearly pretty good and raced regularly. As usual I got hammered in the points race, having not elected to ride for the team in the sprint and the time trial.

When it came to the elimination race I thought I would really have a go. The race started slowly and I just decided to break away. One other rider came with me and we stayed away and out of the elimination battles for most of the race. But eventually we were dragged back by those few remaining and I managed to last one further lap before being eliminated myself. Not a brilliant result but not bad for me and great fun and all the more satisfying knowing I had changed the nature of the race by doing what I did in the first lap.

My time trialling dominated, though, and most weekends and up to one evening a week would see me competing, slowly although far from surely, reducing my personal bests over both my chosen 25-mile distance and the much shorter 10-mile trials.

Testing traditions

Many people in cycling refer to time trialling as 'testing' and really that's just what a time trial is: a test of your speed against the clock. It is one of the most traditional forms of cycle racing and known on the Continent as the 'race of truth'. There really is nowhere to hide. It's just you and your bike riding against the elements and the terrain in the fastest possible time.

It is lonely. You turn up, sign on, get ready, warm up, ride to the start, queue with other riders who seldom talk – nerves and concentration have kicked in long ago. Then there is the push-off and the pain begins. It lasts for as long as you take.

Riders usually start at 1-minute intervals and the rider in front is called your 'minute man'. Catch him and that's at least one person you have beaten. On the other hand, if you get caught by the rider a minute behind you then that's at least one who has beaten you. The problem is that the rider in front might be exceptionally slow. I once took part in a 25-mile event and caught four or five people, but as I neared the finish my computer told me I wasn't on for a particularly fast time. I had been lulled into a false sense of security by passing others who were unusually slower than me and I should have tried harder. I soon realised that the best thing to do is ignore other riders and focus on your own performance.

It's very demoralising being caught by the rider a

A 30-YEAR CYCLE

minute behind you, especially if you are only a mile into the event. In one 10-mile time trial this happened to me. The women's national time trial champion started off that minute behind me. I just couldn't believe she caught me so quickly, barely a mile into the race. It was so demoralising I had to work hard to keep my mind on completing the course. I have also been caught not just by the rider a minute behind but by those starting two, three, four and five or more minutes later. Then you know you are on for a bad day and totally outclassed.

After you cross over the finish line the pain ebbs away. You ride back to your car and repeat almost everything you did before the event in reverse, handing your number in for a free cup of tea and if you are lucky some free cake. Then you can hang around to see the riders' times posted on a large scoreboard, sometimes projected onto a large screen. Unless I think I am in with a chance of a handicap prize I normally get off home. The results are all on the Internet within hours anyway.

Prize money is limited and there aren't often prize ceremonies. Any prizes or winnings are usually sent in the post. I think time trialling or 'testing' is probably the ultimate solitary sport. Granted, there are team time trials, but to get two, three or even four riders together takes some doing and unless you are all very good and prepare for the events they are not easy to ride.

Most people, when I say that I ride time trials, have no idea what I mean. Maybe the description above will help. Some however do say, 'Ah, you are one of those guys with a weird pointy helmet.' I sheepishly admit I am.

It took me a long time to summon up the courage to wear a so-called 'pointy helmet' as I do think they look ridiculous and aren't the sort of thing you should really

Testing traditions

wear until you get pretty good. At my level, the aerodynamic benefit they give is probably negligible, especially because it is so easy to ride with your head down and therefore have the point tilting upwards like a shark's fin, which is likely to be causing more drag.

Although I would have liked road racing to be my main interest, time trialling is a really good alternative. It suits my style of riding and most of all my inability to recover from the sudden changes in pace that take place in mass start events; reacting to attacks or sprinting out of corners. It also suits family life. Traditionally time trials are nearly always held in the early morning so I can get up early, ride in an event and sometimes be back at home before anyone in the household is even out of bed. On a couple of occasions, when the event has been local, I have made it home and gone back to bed as though nothing has happened.

The reason for early starts has changed a little over the years. In the early days of the sport most time trials were held in secret lest the police find out – racing on open roads was banned. Now it's due to the volume of traffic. We have to race and get it over with before Joe Public gets up and out.

On some courses, held on quieter roads, afternoon starts are common, but most events commence at 8 am and some as early as 6.30 or 7 am. This can be convenient, although the need to get up early, eat breakfast and travel to an event destroys the thought of going out the night before. There was a time when I would shake off a late night, even if it involved drinking. Now I just can't. My view is that it's no good spending lots of time training to then throw it away with a night out. I plan my events so I don't have to miss out, but sometimes a sacrifice has to be made.

A 30-YEAR CYCLE

In a 10-mile TT on the A31 near Farnham.

There are other issues relating to early starts, of course; it can be pretty cold, even in summer, and on some occasions there can be early morning mist or fog. I once rode in an event where the visibility was so poor I feared for my safety. I always ride with a flashing red light on the rear of my bike; it's recommended by the sports governing body and mandatory for some events. This usually gives some feeling of security, but on this particular occasion I was totally spooked about being hit by a motorist. My mind was on this and I didn't perform well. Also the visor on my helmet misted up so I couldn't see. It's in those kinds of conditions that I question my sanity and after that particular experience I did resolve on two things: I would not ride in heavy rain or fog.

Luckily I am a 'morning person' and getting up at 5 am doesn't bother me, but I do have a rule. If I would have to get up when the clock is still showing a time before 5 am, I don't enter the race. That is way too early, even for me.

Another throwback to a dark age when time trials had to be held in secret is the course codes that are used. In those days, so that participants knew where to meet and which course they would be riding, a system of codes was established. Even now, for the whole of the UK, all courses have a letter prefix which denotes which geographical region they are in and then two numbers, one usually being the course number and the other the course distance. Any frequent time trialist will therefore still need a codebook to effectively work out where the course is. This comes in the form of an annual handbook, although now the events and course codes are also on the Internet. For the area where I live all the courses have an 'H' prefix, whereas the course I first did my 25-mile sub-hour time on, being in the Midlands, has a 'K' prefix. It does seem a bit weird and also secretive, especially to a newcomer, but in fact the system works very well.

Sadly, new courses are not created very often, mainly due to traffic levels and modern road layouts. Each year there is often a reduction in the number of courses available due to excessive traffic making them dangerous or new road layouts and even traffic lights making them unsuitable for racing.

On the issue of traffic lights, there are more than a few courses I know that do have pedestrian-activated lights

A 30-YEAR CYCLE

on them. Generally these don't cause a problem, especially due to the fact the courses are used in the early morning when few people are around. But then there is the odd dog walker who can seriously ruin a good time or even naughty kids who revel in holding up a time trialist riding flat out. Most lights are policed by event marshals to ensure that competitors don't go through on red, which, sadly, does happen occasionally. Luckily I haven't had my moral fibre tested by a red light! Although I like to think I would stop.

In my first season back, I was involved in an investigation into an incident where a rider had apparently narrowly missed a pedestrian who had pressed the button at a traffic light controlled crossing and thought it was safe to cross. I was eliminated from enquiries based on my start time and when I had been logged at the turn. The rider who appeared to be guilty claimed he couldn't have been at the crossing at the time of the incident as he had 'pulled his rear wheel over while out of the saddle sprinting away from the turn'. A likely story; if he had done this I would have passed him and clearly I hadn't. Breaking the law and endangering a member of the public to get a good time, even a PB, just isn't worth it in my view.

That crossing now has a marshal at all events with the threat of disqualification and disciplinary action for any rider if caught, to stop any temptation to ignore a red light, swerve around a pedestrian and press on. I dread approaching it in case a member of the public appears and presses the button. Pedestrian lights often change to red very quickly and the thought of having to lamp the brakes on at full tilt doesn't fill me with glee, let alone what it would do for lightweight racing tyres.

I love the UK time trialling scene. It is, I believe,

Testing traditions

unique in the world of cycling. No other country practises this form of the sport in the same way. Although time trials have become a firm fixture of major stage races like the Tour de France and Giro d'Italia, they are not the same, usually held over variable terrain and on a circuit.

The traditional British time trial is held on a fast, often fairly flat dual carriageway, although the really fast courses tend to be over undulating terrain. It is no great surprise that events on courses that have a reputation for being conducive to fast times are often oversubscribed with entries. Most courses are referred to as 'out and back', and that's just what they are: out in one direction, turn at a roundabout and then back the other way. Some have a strategic downhill start and a longer outward leg so that conveniently the hill doesn't have to be climbed on the way back. I like those!

Wind can play a major part in time trialling. Due to the out and back nature of the courses it is quite common to 'headbang' into wind on one leg and then have a tailwind on the other. There are times when I have had a terrible time into wind on the way out and then 'sailed' back with a tailwind – the average speeds for each leg being substantially different.

The courses with more traffic can be pretty frightening and there is a need to keep your wits about you, although some riders relish the benefit of the drafting effect lorries and larger vehicles can provide. The early starts help. Even at quieter times the inherent danger is always there due to the fact that cycle racing and motor vehicles really don't mix. One mistake and that can be it. I remember well a guy from my youth called Anthony; he was always friendly and turned up with his parents. I never really talked to him much but we always said hello. He made the fatal error one day of doing a U-turn just after the finish of a time trial. That was it for him; I understood he was killed instantly. To this day, after every finish where a U-turn is possible and required I always look back again and again and remember what happened to Anthony. Many courses ban such manoeuvres.

There are now a growing number of events set on courses that are far from flat and also based on a circuit. These are referred to as sporting courses. I like the idea of these as they are on quieter roads and really challenging in their nature. But like road racing circuits, they don't suit me; I much prefer the faster flatter traditional courses and just have to put up with the obvious risks.

Some of the best riders in the sport have come from a time trialling background of early starts, out and back courses, tea and cakes. It really is where the grass roots of cycling are and is pretty much unique to the UK. Long may it continue.

Old gits
(retire immediately)

'Old cyclists never die, they just get dropped!' I saw this humorous statement on a mature cyclist's T-shirt and it probably has some truth in it. But many older cyclists I have met are still very capable on a bike well into their sixties, seventies and even eighties. Some stand out and are worth a mention.

I first met Dave whilst riding to the start of a local club time trial. I thought he looked as though he was in his late fifties. He asked me how long I had been a member of Newbury Road Club. I said, 'Oh, about ten months.' He told me he had been a member since 1946. He didn't mean it as a put down but it felt like it. Over the next few months I got to know him a bit, mainly because he was still competing in time trials. When I found out he was over eighty I was in shock, especially as the first time I had competed against him he had beaten me by nearly two minutes! His aim was to win events based on the standard time for his age and the far superior time he could achieve. More often than not, he covered his petrol money!

It took me two seasons to get the better of Dave. When I did, I felt very sad. It felt like I had beaten him, albeit by the smallest of margins, not due to my improvement but really due to his natural decline as an octogenarian. Someone who can turn in 24- or 25-minute

A 30-YEAR CYCLE

10-mile time trials at that age must have more than his fair share of natural ability. Not only that, it must take a lot of application and perseverance, especially as I gather he had to fight back at least once from a major accident in his seventies.

Dave 'hung up his wheels' in 2012. He even sold his bike immediately to ensure he didn't go back on his word. That season I stood alongside him after a 10-mile TT near Farnham. I had beaten him probably for only the second time and even then by only 30 seconds. He told me then that this would be his last season, that he had started racing in the year of the 1948 London Olympics and that now, at the time of the 2012 London Olympics, it was time to bow out. A racing career of 64 years and even that day, yet again, he won the handicap prize based on his veteran's standard time.

'Do you remember Charlie?' said Dad on the phone.

'Yes, of course – he used to come on club runs,' I replied.

'He's still riding,' said Dad with more than an element of surprise in his voice.

He had called me to say there was a piece in his local paper about Charlie and the fact he was still riding a bike at 90 years old. According to the article he planned on keeping going until he was at least 100!

Charlie seemed old even when I was 13 or 14 years old. But I guess anyone over 30 does to a teenager. While I had left cycling he had kept on going and was still knocking out the miles. I only learnt recently that he died at the end of 2012 and, you guessed it, he was out on his bike at the time – at the age of 92. Not bad at all.

Old gits (retire immediately)

'Mick Ives? You two should retire immediately – he is bloody ancient.' And before I could get a word in, 'How embarrassing. I could never let that happen!'

That was my dad giving me his forthright views after a two-up time trial Simon and I rode in early 2010. It was only 21 miles but we had clocked 1:00:09. Mick and his teammate had put in a very creditable 49:57. We could hardly believe that the margin he and his 64-year-old teammate had over two late-forty somethings would be so great. But it was. And this experience became the start of my education about the ability of older guys to beat me by immense time differences.

I also had a ride one winter Sunday with a fellow Newbury Road Club member who, like me, had been brought up in Staffordshire, so we had something in common. He even rode a Brian Rourke bike from Tunstall, Stoke-on-Trent. I had no idea how old he was and thought he could be in his late fifties. It turned out he was nearly 70. He was clearly still pretty fit and like most riders of his vintage turned up without a water bottle. I think to them having a drink on a ride is a sign of weakness. Even though in my youth it had been quite normal to ride for a couple of hours or so without drinking, these days there is so much advice around about keeping hydrated that I was surprised he had no drink. He wouldn't accept one from me either.

I was expecting an easy ride but for some reason he forced the pace and we ended up with the sort of behaviour best left to those many years younger – half-wheeling each other incessantly and continually increasing the pace. This wasn't a problem for me and I stuck at it, also riding hard when it became my turn to lead into the wind. I didn't particularly enjoy the ride, though, as it wasn't the sociable morning out I had assumed we

A 30-YEAR CYCLE

would have. At the end he even sprinted for the last village sign and I certainly let him know who was boss then, winning by a few lengths.

Afterwards he blamed me for making it a hard ride, the insinuation being that I had given an older man a hard time. That's a bit rich, I thought; all I had done was respond to his own pace setting. No one would have been happier than me to have ambled along and talked about common acquaintances and shared experiences.

You have to watch these old guys; they can certainly give you a run for your money and more than knock your ego. It's that age-old competitive streak that doesn't leave some people. And I'm glad it doesn't.

It was all over the news last year about a 100-year-old French cyclist, Robert Marchand, riding 100 kilometres on a velodrome at an average speed of 23 km/h (that's 14.3 mph). When I think back, I struggled to ride at that pace when I first returned to the sport as a 47-year-old!

I am convinced that cycling can be the elixir of life for some. These are just a few examples of those I have met or heard about who still turn the pedals at a grand old age; I wish them all well and only hope in time I will become one of them.

Things that cyclists do

To some of my Étape teammates, even wearing Lycra was effeminate and they certainly weren't going to shave their legs. In some cases their rugby playing heritage probably set a very firm stance on this.

On a particular ride when one of them noticed my smooth legs he exclaimed, 'You fucking homosexual.' Why leg shaving and my sexuality should be linked I don't know and in fact I know loads of gay blokes who have hairy legs, but this slightly portly, very ex-rugby player clearly had a real problem with it!

I had shaved my legs for the first time in nearly 30 years in preparation for my first road race, anxious to look the part if nothing else. They had been hidden for much of the day by my leg warmers in view of the cold start on a late September morning. As the sun came out and it warmed up, off came the covers and out came my smooth legs. No one noticed at first but when one man did it was as though I had really offended him. He even went on to tell my wife I wasn't the man he'd thought I was. I never enquired to find out what he thought I was prior to shaving my legs!

There was much discussion about leg shaving before we left to do the Étape. Steve and Pete were to remain definite 'no's but Simon kept quiet about it and did shave for our first event together, the two-up time trial. He kept them that way for the Étape but they grew hairy again at the end of the season, just like mine did.

A 30-YEAR CYCLE

At some times, I think the discussion on leg shaving has by far overtaken any other when cycling is the topic. People seem to like to talk about it due to its apparent oddity. I don't think any other sport has something so peculiar associated with its participants. In my experience, girls are really fascinated by it. After the question 'Why?', when they don't get an answer that makes any sense, the conversation drifts on to how you do it.

'Why don't you wax?'

'How far up do you shave?'

These are at least two of the questions I've been asked. They never seem to realise it's really just a perfunctory thing for a cyclist. It's not really about vanity (though some would say it is and cycling does attract its fair share of posers!) or getting the smoothest finish. It is just a thing cyclists do.

It was never an issue when I was younger but as a middle-aged man, I used to feel very self-conscious about my bare legs when wearing shorts in the warm sun after, say, a day's skiing or at a summer barbecue. I still get comments now from even our closest friends. Others who don't know you give strange looks.

I think there is a saving grace and a reason why cyclists do get away with shaven legs without been looked upon as potential transvestites or some kind of weirdo. If you have 'cyclists'' legs then they may be clean-shaven, even smooth and tanned, but the mass of varicose veins standing out and the bulging muscles don't look feminine or at all attractive.

It appears that it is totally OK for footballers, those guys on *Strictly Come Dancing* (and that must definitely be for vanity) and the like to shave their chests but weird for cyclists to shave their legs. I would never dream of shaving my chest – although it had to be shaved for my heart operation. In both cases, chest and legs, although there are many reasons given, I think the prime driver is probably vanity or at least a wish to conform with others in their sport.

I hear now from a doctor friend of mine that the current trend for young women is to shave their pubes! In fact body hair generally seems off the menu for many, male or female. But for cyclists it is just their legs. I find it amusing to see them often pulling up to start a race with a few days' stubble on the chin but cleanly shaven on the limbs that do all the work.

So be it.

Lycra is another thing. Everyone now recognises the term MAMIL (Middle-Aged Man in Lycra). Some guys take on what my father called the Max Wall (if you can remember him) look with portly torsos supported by thin Lycra-clad legs. Few, if any, can look good in this kit and it is best to stay on the bike as much as you can if out and about in Lycra.

I think that what can be ridiculous is when, to look like their favourite pro team rider or perhaps because they got them cheap, guys wear leg wear in any colour other than black. White, red, blue or even green leg warmers and training tights look bloody awful and make for a court jester-like appearance rather than that of a serious cyclist. Even the pros in teams who unfortunately have sponsors that necessitate the use of non-black kit often look silly.

Wearing a Lycra skinsuit for the first time is a bit weird. It leaves nothing to the imagination and shows all of the natural curves of the body and of course everything that sticks out. If you're a man, it always pays to check where a certain appendage is placed. Otherwise, there can be an embarrassing moment when the lady at the signing-

A 30-YEAR CYCLE

in desk gets a full view of your manhood's clear outline through the Lycra.

Having a pee is also an art form. Usually there are two methods, depending upon the style of suit. Some suits have a zipped front and the zip goes low enough to allow easy access, especially if you are well endowed. If not, or when the zip is not low enough, the only other way is to roll up a leg of the suit and pull you know what out. This can be very painful, especially if your pubes get caught in the Lycra. Any last dribbles also show up long after.

One thing you really shouldn't do is wear white Lycra. Why? Well, it becomes see-through when it's wet, as is often the case in the UK. It may be OK for

In the white skin suit and it's raining again!

some pro teams that mainly operate in the warmer climes of Europe but is potentially a major faux pas at home. This fact was bought into sharp relief for me and Simon when very early on in my return to racing we rode the two-up time trial together. Not to be outgunned by the competition even before we started, legs were shaved and I managed to get hold of two very cheap skinsuits. You've guessed it, they were cheap because ... they were white.

The alarming thing about the suits was that even when dry they were barely opaque. When wet, that was it – more akin to wearing cling film! They would have looked great on a page three model but were bloody awful on middle-aged blokes. I have only worn mine once since and it fucking rained again.

It is often easy to plot the course of a new cyclist's career, especially in this Wiggo era. They start off, as we did, in baggy shorts on mountain bikes. Before long the Lycra takes hold in garish colours. In my view the main reason is that people want to look the part but it's also because the kit available these days is well designed and fit for purpose, and that's the key thing: 'purpose'. If you're wearing it elsewhere it looks ridiculous.

Winding back the clock, wool was the fabric of choice. It was warm and fitted well. Problem was it soon went baggy and when wet became awful to wear. You still see some old guys wearing it; they clearly just can't face the male ballet dancer look.

Just as it is in football, replica team kit is a big thing in cycling. It always has been, even when I started all those years ago. Then it was sophisticated and unknown Italian trade teams that were de rigueur. Now it's more household brands like Sky, Garmin or Radioshack. I think it's great and can transform the look of a middle-

A 30-YEAR CYCLE

aged guy, providing he isn't too overweight, to that of a continental pro.

The one thing I don't agree with, though, is those who succumb to wearing the hallowed yellow, green, pink, red and white polka dot world championship jerseys or Team GB kit. The right to wear these should be earned. Nothing is worse than seeing a fat guy wearing one of these while resting his gut on the crossbar of his expensive Italian road bike. You do see them, though. 'All the gear, no idea,' as my older son says.

Now of course female cyclists can look great in Lycra, but only a few do and you will know which ones when they come past you!

As I have already mentioned, for racing in time trials, so-called 'pointy helmets' are in vogue due to their aerodynamic properties. I was very self-conscious about mine at first. Even now I am more embarrassed when people ask if I wear a pointy helmet than when questioned whether I shave my legs. In order to remain aerodynamic the trick with a pointy helmet is to keep the pointy bit as low as possible, almost touching the upper back (which should be flat) if you can manage it. It takes some getting used to and hurts. What I found helped was to train on my turbo with my TT bike, down in the aerodynamic position, so at least the body gets used to being in a strange and unnatural place.

'Why do you wear your socks over your shoes?'
'Can't you afford shoes?'
Ha ha, I always think.

One of the ways of keeping your feet warm on cool days, not to mention keeping your cycling shoes clean, is to buy a pair of specifically designed cycling oversocks. They normally have holes pre-cut for cleats and at the heel. I agree they look stupid but at least they are functional and the Belgians manage to make them look cool and trendy. So, why can't we?

Some cyclists collect bikes. What is often said to be the formula for the number of bikes you need is:

$$n + 1$$
*(n = the number of bikes currently owned
+ 1 refers to the next one you need and will soon buy)*

There was a debate amongst our friends a few years back, about the machine referred to as a winter bike. All thought this was very amusing. As I became more serious again about the sport and planned a full training schedule which often involved long sessions out on the winter roads, I convinced myself that I couldn't possibly take my expensive carbon road bike out in all weathers. I basically bought a cheaper version of the same bike, put mudguards and lights on, and that was it: the winter bike. It was the bike I didn't mind getting dirty or feel compelled to clean after every ride.

Before long our garage, like those of many cyclists (the serious ones, at least), was full of bikes. I now only have four, with a few frames sprinkled about and no end of wheels. I often wonder how it all came about – having four bikes, that is – but it has recently been made very clear to me through my younger son's involvement in the sport.

He started with a road bike, naturally. Track racing followed, so that was bike number two. He had a go at BMX riding, bike number three. Then there were opportunities to ride mountain bikes and even cyclo-cross. He has a mountain bike but I drew the line at cyclo-cross. A

A 30-YEAR CYCLE

fifth bike would have been taking the piss, not to mention filling an already crammed garage. The cyclo-cross season is so short and it's such bloody hard work that I knew he wouldn't like it anyway.

While on the subject of bikes, something in vogue for serious cyclists now is the bike fitting. Lots of people offer this service: an opportunity to spend well over £100 on having your bike set up specifically to suit your body. I was told getting the right position could be worth another 10 watts of power. That was good enough for me; I made a booking and spent the best part of half a day on the bike fitting. I admit that we changed a lot and the new position, lower handlebars and a higher saddle, did feel right. Did it give me more power, though? Well, I have to say no! I haven't really noticed any appreciable difference at all in that.

A whole industry has emerged around bike fitting. The most fanatical cyclists can also spend time in wind tunnels perfecting their position on the bike to ensure the optimum aerodynamic benefit. To do this you really do have to be serious about (and good at) time trials, to the point where you really are looking for those marginal gains. And prepared to spend thousands!

One of my mates spent thousands of pounds in the wind tunnel. Although he knew what position to hold while in there, he admitted that when he was riding on the open road and especially when competing he couldn't bear the pain of staying in that optimum aerodynamic position. I can't really see the point in knowing how to be positioned and then not being able to adopt it.

For all cyclists but particularly newcomers, using cleats and clip-on pedals is worrying for the first time.

Things that cyclists do

Will you be able to get your foot out when you stop? I have witnessed many funny moments with people falling off at slow speed still locked into their pedals. It's not only embarrassing but it hurts too. One of the particular hazards is when you are struggling up a particularly steep hill. At slow speed all you need to do is lose your balance and then that's it, over you go onto the tarmac.

While off the bike we also teeter about in cycling shoes with cleats that are clearly fit for purpose and slip neatly onto the bike pedals but are bloody hopeless for walking in, often making the wearer slip and skid all over the place. Owners of village halls, often used for race HQs, don't like them either. Apparently they can damage their pristine floors, so as if you're entering a house-proud owner's home, it's off with the shoes to walk about in socks.

Don't let your cleats get too worn either. I know of at least two people who didn't notice their cleats had worn down due to excessive walking on them to the point they wouldn't stay in the pedals under pressure. Both of them got out of the saddle for a sprint and ended up going over the bars. One sadly broke his collarbone and lost some teeth.

I have found that any group of cyclists when together will race each other given half the chance. With any group of guys there is always some competitive tension. Put them on bikes and sooner or later nature kicks in and a 'race' of sorts will take place. This may be based on who gets to the top of a hill first, who can be first home, even a sprint for a village sign, but believe me, it will take place. People just like competing and bike riding will bring it out in them.

A 30-YEAR CYCLE

One of the phenomena of the current bike riding scene is the sportive. They didn't exist when I was young. The nearest we had was the reliability trial. I loved these but for some reason I don't love sportives. I just don't see the point in paying to ride a route I could ride for free anyway or in driving some distance to ride a particular route when I can just get on my bike and ride from my garage door. It is nice to enjoy a good ride with others but not hundreds or even thousands; that spoils it for me.

The reliability trials were very similar to sportives but different in that they were really all about road racers getting fit for the season ahead. They were a test of a rider's current fitness level and therefore had a real purpose. The first one I took part in was to Nantwich in Cheshire. It was a circular route of 100 kilometres. Basically it was the closest thing you could get to racing and we covered the whole route in 3.5 hours.

I probably did this event three times and always enjoyed it immensely. It was timed but the organisation was fairly relaxed and I remember a couple of drinks stops and getting time-checked en route. We even got a certificate for our efforts. The nice thing also was that there were really only a handful of people taking part in the event, probably 50 or so, whereas today in sportives there can be hundreds or even thousands of participants. The event in question appears, from what I see on the 'web', to still take place every March.

Another memorable reliability trial was known as the Montgomery and back. I rode this when I was about 15 or 16. My parents had no idea, that Sunday morning when I got up at 5 am, of where I was headed or what I would be doing. The start was at a grubby transport café on the A5 near Cannock, a far cry from the roadside facilities we have these days.

Things that cyclists do

A small group of us, of which I was the youngest, cycled over to the start in the early morning mist and light rain. I was both excited and apprehensive, not surprising given the distance was 120 miles. That was further than I had ever been on a bike, probably by 30–40 miles or so. A foolish endeavour, perhaps, but it was ridden in a very relaxed manner.

We set off with a large group of guys who were much older. The route was mainly on the A5, which would be impossible today, in view of the amount of traffic, but it was acceptably quiet in those days. The weather wasn't kind to us. Light rain turned heavier and then became sleet or snow for a while but we pressed on, riding two abreast. Turns at the front of the group were hard, into wind, but thankfully brief. I can still vividly remember when our group was caught by a much faster one at some stage during the day. It was full of young racing guys and contained a national champion of the time. I watched in awe as they raced past and disappeared into the gloom while I just hung on in there.

The day is a bit of a blur really, not because it has been lost in the mists of time, but because at some stage I must have entered a state of delirium, similar to the state I've experienced running marathons. This almost anaesthetises the body and enables suffering beyond normal levels of endurance.

I completed the ride. Quite how I made it home that night I just don't know. All I do know is that I was in a state beyond tiredness but somehow I managed to function normally and my parents didn't even ask what I had been up to. They were probably surprised I had been out for so long but there was no concern. That all changed, of course, when I started hanging around with girls!

A 30-YEAR CYCLE

In the seventies and eighties no one wore helmets, when training anyway. They were mandatory for racing on road and track events. The protection they offered then was pretty minimal. Luckily I never put mine to the test. All it was made of was some padded leather strips with little in the way of structure or reinforcement.

In time trials they weren't required and still aren't. If it weren't for the aerodynamic benefits, particularly of the 'pointy' helmets, I don't think many of those competing in time trials would even bother with them now. But, given the busy roads we race on, that could be considered downright dangerous.

I must admit I don't like wearing one now, especially as I rode for so many miles without one in my youth. It's that feeling of speeding along with the wind in your hair and the freedom this conveys that just can't be replicated with a 'bed pan', as my dad called them, on your head. These days, though, I wouldn't go out without one. I did have a nasty bump of the head in my twenties while not wearing a helmet and now I just feel naked without one.

There is a similar feeling of freedom while skiing, but now ski helmets are in wide use and look like becoming compulsory for insurance cover. It can't be long before cycling follows.

One of the many peculiarities of cyclists is the fads they will often follow relating to training or what they eat. These are often promoted by the cycling publications of the day and more than a few books. More on eating and training later, but cyclists are generally obsessed with their weight although most are at the thinner end of the population's weight spectrum. You don't see many fat cyclists, not after they have been riding for a while anyway.

With regard to weight, it must be the hills that do it – one thing you don't want to drag uphill is excess weight. There is, of course, no point spending money on a decent bike and then piling on the pounds unless track sprinting is your chosen occupation. One other reason, I am sure, is the common usage of Lycra in the sport. All would agree there is nowhere to hide anything in that stuff and it probably encourages more than a few to keep trimmer than they perhaps would otherwise.

My final comment on cyclists' habits is about nose blowing without using a tissue or handkerchief. This is brought about by the method most used on the bike: hold one nostril closed using a finger and blow hard down the other one. It is very efficient and of course acceptable when on your own but not nice when others are close and totally disgusting when not on a bike. You know certain riders do it; they are the ones with black smudge marks on their noses, caused by oily hands – often an occupational hazard of bike riding.

Heroes

I had many cycling heroes in my youth. Probably in common with many youngsters at the time and bearing in mind he was still racing when I first started riding, Eddy Merckx was my favourite. I was so excited to meet him and get his autograph at the Ghent six-day event in 1980, shortly after he had retired.

Even today I still collect Eddy Merckx memorabilia and from time to time buy his vintage bike frames. I always planned to build a full retro bike but it hasn't happened yet!

I also followed Bernard Hinault, Francesco Moser and a few others. British star riders were few and far between, nowhere near as prolific as they are now. Also the information flow from the main racing scene in Europe pre-Internet wasn't that good.

In more recent times, I have followed the fortunes of a number of riders, many of them now British and of course a particular American who has since fallen spectacularly from grace in view of his and his team's systematic drug taking.

My only attendance at a cycling event between 1981 and 2010 was at that American's first victory in the Tour de France. It was so exciting to be there but didn't encourage me to ride a bike again. A big contrast with the more recent British successes in the event, which did motivate me greatly. Seeing Wiggo flash past at high speed in a time trial, his upper body rock solid on the bike, made me want to emulate his machine-like style. Never fancied having the sideburns, though.

My only worry now about the heroes of yesteryear is 'did they take drugs or not?' Sadly, I fear many of them probably did. By all accounts it was endemic then and indeed has been until fairly recently. I think the kids of today really do have some role models to follow. We didn't really, although we were fairly unaware of the goings on at the time.

My doubts about the heroes I followed have made this chapter the shortest in the book.

The club time warp

Although in the lead-up to doing the Étape we had formed our own home village-based cycling club, the Wayfarers Wheelers, this didn't last long, as a formal entity anyway. We did secure a couple of local companies to sponsor us and had some smart kit produced, but the other guys weren't really interested in or committed to racing so there seemed no point continuing. They still ride in the kit today, though.

The Wayfarers Wheelers l'Etape Team. L–R: Simon Holland, The Author, Pete Dunmore, Steve Suttie and either side, our sponsors Neil and Christine Leah of C&N Sales.

The club time warp

As I was keen to race after my enjoyable but brief and unsuccessful experiences in both road races and time trials, I finally succumbed and joined a proper cycling club for the first time since 1981. Previously I had belonged to Velo Club Ventoux, a small group of road racing cyclists, including the local bike shop owner, which had formed to commemorate the untimely death of British pro Tom Simpson on the upper slopes of Mont Ventoux in 1967. Then I had joined a more traditional club based in a town near where I lived, Brereton Wheelers.

My view has always been that it is only right to support a football club that is local to where you live or were brought up. Supporting a club where you have no personal connection makes no sense to me, even if that personal connection means having an allegiance with a team that are not in the upper flight, in my case either Stoke City or Wolverhampton Wanderers.

So to me, it made sense to join a cycling club that was based near where I now live. There were a few choices as although the nearest town is Newbury, our village of Highclere is actually in Hampshire and is also near to Andover. This meant there were three clubs that I could join based on geographic principles: Newbury Road Club, North Hampshire Road Club or Andover Wheelers.

I had already got to know some of the guys at Newbury RC as I had ridden a few of their club time trials. They seemed to have a full calendar of events and were local enough, so I sent off my money and membership application.

I guess, though, that I wasn't looking for anything social and although I thought it would be good to go on club runs again, I have to date only been on one. My main motivation was being part of a group of guys who

A 30-YEAR CYCLE

raced with all the necessary regulatory body affiliations.

I had realised long before I joined that things had changed little in the club scene in over 30 years. It was like I was in a late-seventies, early-eighties time warp. Right from my first encounter with the guys at Newbury, I immediately felt at home, as though the years had just melted away.

Like most cycling groups I have come across, I didn't find them particularly friendly. Most of them were a lot older than me and had been club members for many years. They would regularly talk about the need to attract new members, but to me it was quite obvious they weren't going to 'charm' people into joining. The main attraction for those who developed an interest in the sport was probably the camaraderie of the club run. Only a relatively small group of club members actually raced and then the main focus was on time trialling, which of course is probably one of the most alien forms of the sport to a newcomer and hardly sociable.

Compared to my experiences of 30 years before in the Midlands many of the club stereotypes were still evident, I found, and I recognised a significant number of them:

> The club coach – a fount of all knowledge and pivotal member around which the club revolved;
> The racing star – slightly aloof and dedicated to his craft, with a record of performances well beyond the reach of other club members;
> The guy who organised club runs and the like – who I sensed you really didn't want to cross (there was one we called the Ayatollah; he has a couple of mentions elsewhere);
> The friendly one – not particularly good at racing but always there to answer questions and give useful advice;

The club time warp

The girl – oh yes, they existed even then – always good-looking, at least compared to the blokes, and far too bloody good, putting many male racers to shame;

The club comedian – always there to take the piss;

The rich fucker who turned up occasionally to show off his tan from spending his early retirement somewhere in Southern Europe;

The cycling club equivalent of the village idiot – I knew one who was christened 'Brains' after a character in the then-popular children's TV series *Top Cat*. His real name was Andrew and he was a lovely guy, strong on a bike too. I met him again recently and reminisced over old times;

The club poser – we used to have one who rode a team issue TI-Raleigh bike in matching kit – until he had a bad crash, hitting a raised manhole cover;

The old geezer – often a former racer still turning out good performances. Just don't get into half-wheeling this guy. And finally:

The gobby one – a know-all only interested in himself who never shuts up. I remember a guy who also used to whistle as we rode along in the chain gang. I think there is nothing more annoying than someone knocking out a familiar tune while you are suffering.

The rest blended into the background. Interestingly, almost the only stereotype missing from Newbury Road Club was the local bike shop owner. I later found out that he had been a member but had left with a few others to form a club more focused on racing some years before. Again parallels with the Velo Club Ventoux, my first ever club.

I remember well the first time I met some of the above characters at a club time trial. I rolled up, said hello and nobody acknowledged me. Silence! I paid my entry fee, signed on and collected my number, all without really

A 30-YEAR CYCLE

any communication from those running the event. People were talking and joking in small groups of two or three but none seemed interested in me, a new guy. I just hung around on my own until it was time to warm up and then to start.

Even when I did turn up to start, my cheery greetings to the pusher-off and timekeeper were greeted with silence. Oh well, I thought. I signed up to race, not to have a chit-chat. I have since pulled up at countless time trials with many other clubs and more often than not very little is said at the start. Sometimes I get what seems like a begrudging 'good morning' and maybe if I'm lucky 'good luck' as the pusher-off lets go.

It often makes me think I am not taking it seriously enough and should roll up not saying a word, complete with so-called 'race face' on and in the zone, ready to ride a wave of pain for the allotted miles. A complete non-speaking part.

With my experience at the start line of the club time trial, I was back. This time in a layby on the A4 to the east of Newbury, but it could have been the A449 or A51 up in Staffordshire back in 1978 or 1979. The cars going past would have been Ford Cortinas and Vauxhall Vivas rather than BMWs and Audis. There would have been no Lycra and everyone would have been on road bikes with no aero bars, but otherwise it was eerily the same.

I am always wary of pushers-off at time trials. One I remember for all the wrong reasons was a guy named Carl; we knew each other and had ridden a few events together. That particular night he took on the usual persona of a pusher-off and chose to be distant, not even acknowledging me. I think I had always beaten him in road races and at time trials; that thought had been far from my mind until he briefly held on to me with 30 seconds to go

The club time warp

and then for no apparent reason let go. I immediately fell into the road, the whole experience made worse by the fact cars were passing perilously close as I scrambled to release myself from my toe straps and get up. Why he did it I had no idea; he only muttered a belated 'sorry'. As you can imagine, I rode with anger that night, cursing Carl, the grazes on my right leg and the scratches on my bike. I never talked to him again. A bit extreme, perhaps, but I couldn't forgive that 'blunder'.

Club AGMs haven't changed either. Now, as then, they are only attended by a few and I usually get the feeling that they don't really want to be there. There is a divide between those who race and those who ride recreationally on club runs, the latter a growing number who have never raced; both have a place in the club but have very different needs.

There is always a lack of volunteers for the various posts on the club committee. That's probably true for any club or organisation, not just one focused on cycling. The danger is that once you have accepted a role it will be hard to give it up, at least for a few years anyway, until a gullible replacement raises his or her hand. When the request goes out at the meeting it's like the first time you enter an active auction room, becoming statuesque and looking at the floor in order to avoid making any commitment to purchase.

Topics that I consider worthy of debate aren't dwelt upon, but then the most trivial are. At a recent AGM it was the subject of club kit; someone from the floor suggested a re-design, the reason being that our club initials are NRC.

'People keep asking me why Newbury Rugby Club ride bikes,' she said.

'It does spell it out on the front,' replied another.

A 30-YEAR CYCLE

A long debate followed, after which 'no change' was agreed.

There was another recent comment about the club's centenary that 'would be coming up soon'; I noted that on the club letterhead it said 'founded in 1925', so we were at the time 13 years away. Sadly many members who were in the room probably won't be around for the occasion. Perhaps this is part of the mindset of a cyclist: they just don't believe they will ever fade away. That's why so many of them look and behave like they are at least ten years younger than they are.

If you meet the members of a cycling club out on their bikes or in a social setting, one thing that becomes immediately apparent is that here is an area of society where being overweight let alone obesity, doesn't exist. In an era when fast food prevails, in its many formats, it is safe to say there are no fat cyclists. In a sport where at all levels the participants can easily be identified by their gaunt and lean appearance, even the slightly overweight stand out. Perhaps a national programme of bike riding might cure our current malaise in the UK where I gather over 20% of the population are said to be obese.

I understand that even ambulances today have to be kitted out to deal with the size of the likely passengers, assuming the paramedics can get them in there in the first place. No such problem with cyclists; they can be picked up with ease. But although there is space for the often damaged bike too, it's not allowed. Don't even think about it; there is no way your bike will be going with you. I have pleaded and failed. If you need a journey in an ambulance your bike is most likely to be the least of your worries, even if it is your racing machine, your pride and joy.

The club time warp

Although other social events have gone by the wayside, fortunately the club annual dinner is still held and is one of the few chances to interact. We haven't yet found a way to have a 'virtual' presentation of the club trophies.

Thirty years on, the club dinner hasn't changed. Some get dressed up, some don't bother, some have no idea. I think cyclists are so programmed into what they wear on a bike, which has to be functional, that they don't know what to do when dressing for normal life. Some wear a dinner suit; what's that all about? The older guys wear sports jackets and ties and for most of us anything goes. Looking around the room at the last dinner I went to, it would have been hard to work out what the particular group of people was. We could have been bird watchers as much as cyclists for all a casual onlooker would have thought.

A few bring their wives. Most don't – the last place their other half, mine included, would want to be is with a group of cyclists, talking about cycling and nothing but.

These aren't really drunken and are definitely not raucous affairs as no one really drinks. The young ones and serious racing types are thinking about how it could adversely affect their performance and the older ones griping about the cost of even the cheapest house wine.

Back in the eighties they were in my experience nearly all-male affairs and the only females were some long-suffering wives or girlfriends. Now there are thankfully more girls and many of them cyclists too. Hopefully a growing trend given the recent Olympic successes of our female cyclists.

I have very fond memories of the club runs of my youth to Bridgnorth, Ashbourne, Market Drayton and Consall Forge. I started when I was only 13. My parents had no

A 30-YEAR CYCLE

idea of what I was up to and were very trusting of those I was riding with. Nowadays there is no way I would let my kids go alone with a group of older guys on long rides.

The club run then was also a day-long affair. Nowadays they are generally much shorter and although a café stop is included, it's only for a snack, with the riders being back around lunchtime. The distances we covered in the past took a lot longer and the stop was for lunch before a long ride home.

There used to be a time when the club run was populated with riders who had been racers. It was a natural progression as middle age set in and racing became a thing of the past. There was always the opportunity to reminisce over the mid-ride refreshments. Now with an active veteran scene, those with a seemingly unquenchable competitive streak can just keep on competing, and many do. This means they also don't want to take up responsibility for club matters; it takes up valuable time that needs to be used for training.

What is really different in the cycling club of today is the impact of the Internet. The need to hold club meetings has dwindled. Gone are the days when a weekly meet would be held as I was used to in my youth. Now it's a so-called forum on the club website or even Facebook that acts as a channel of social interaction. In many ways it's great – all the benefits of being in touch with fellow club members without having to leave your home. It is still nice to see other like-minded humans every now and again, though.

One of my most memorable experiences as a club cyclist was a trip organised by a group of members of Velo Club Ventoux to the Ghent six-day track race in Belgium. This was both good and bad.

The club time warp

My trip to Ghent at the tender age of 17 was to be my first abroad. I had to get a passport. No one else in my family had one. We had been 'overseas' to Jersey on holidays but you didn't need one for there.

Only five of us made the trip, crammed into an old Ford Cortina. The route took us down the M1 and then in those pre-M25 days around the very congested North Circular Road. For a boy from the Midlands it all felt very alien and busy. After what seemed like an eternity we finally made it to Dover. Problem there was it had become very wet and windy. We checked in but were told there would be a delay to our sailing in view of the strong winds.

Eventually and to our collective surprise, we were called to board. The weather appeared to us to have worsened and rain was lashing down. The excitement of the trip ahead had long disappeared as we expected a long wait at Dover and the weekend was dwindling away.

After boarding, it was decided we would have something to eat. For some reason we behaved like some real big-time Charlies and went for the smart-looking restaurant. Before long we were tucking in to what to us seemed like an exotic French dish, chicken chasseur.

I made it known it wasn't the first time I had enjoyed French cuisine. It was true; we had been served this very dish by my mother some months earlier, courtesy of some ready-made packet-based sauce. What I didn't let on was that there had been a near riot at the dinner table that evening. Both of us kids and my dad complaining about the absence of chips and egg or some other Midlands staple ingredients.

I remember one of the guys commenting, as we tucked in, that the sea conditions weren't too bad after

A 30-YEAR CYCLE

all. Little did he and indeed any of us know we were still inside the outer harbour wall at Dover. By the time we reached open sea we were well into our meal. By then, all hell had broken loose; the ferry was soon pitching and rolling and generally being tossed about in the angry sea.

The meal was over fairly swiftly, washed down with some red wine and beer. I think the staff wanted to get it all over with quickly and close down for the night. The struggle to serve customers in the rough conditions was testing the most experienced waiters.

Trying to walk out of the restaurant was a challenge. We were probably a bit drunk and this made us a little unstable but due to the violent movement of the ferry, we were literally bouncing off the walls as we made our way down the corridor to find some seats.

There were people lying everywhere and the smell of vomit was strong. As we passed doors that led onto the open deck, I noticed they were lashed up with rope in case some idiot decided to go for a walk only to be washed away.

Four of us clubbed together and paid for a cabin in an effort to get some semblance of a comfortable night's sleep. This would prove impossible; soon after we had settled down the first one got up to puke into the cabin sink.

The mixture of wine, beer and food wouldn't stay down long for any of us. I was unfortunate to be the last to answer the inevitable call to liberate my meal. I had been lying face down as the boat moved around erratically; sometimes the pitching of the boat felt as though we would just keep going down. Then we would hit the sea again and the cycle would repeat itself again and again.

The club time warp

As I felt the urgent call to puke I swung out of my bunk. Made it to the sink only to find it completely filled to the brim with my three other colleagues' vomit. There was no time to do anything else but roll up my sleeve and clear the blockage. Luckily for me, some clown had left the plug in. With this removed the sink proved to have the capacity to take my donation.

Bearing in mind the smell in the cabin I decided to go for a walk, or rather a stagger and crawl. The scene was shocking, people lying everywhere, looking awful. I went into the toilet but was beaten back by the odour and the water – or maybe something else – swilling around the floor as the boat rocked from side to side.

We had left home all excited. Now, as day dawned and we left the ferry, all of us were hung over with the after-effects of seasickness and throbbing headaches. The drive to Ghent from Zeebrugge was a quiet one. Luckily no one was sick.

After that very shaky start the weekend was great, the racing exciting and the beer and frites very tasty. I got the chance to meet my hero, Eddy Merckx, who calmly dealt with all those Brits and others who wanted to shake his hand and get an autograph.

After two days and one night of spectating we made our way home across the Channel, thankfully in calm conditions. The drive home was almost uneventful until Dave, our driver at the time, fell asleep at the wheel and we veered onto the hard shoulder. The whole car, woken up by the change in road noise and sound of cats' eyes being hit at speed, yelled at him and he corrected course.

I was sent home from work the next day. Apparently I looked awful and could hardly keep awake. Ever since then I have always liked the cut and thrust of track racing and avidly followed the six-day events in Europe,

A 30-YEAR CYCLE

including London's own Skol beer six-day event until it stopped in the mid-eighties.

One of the best things about club membership for me is being able to race, particularly in the weekly club time trials. I salute those stalwarts of cycling clubs everywhere who put on, in all weathers, a weekly time trial. This is often done by a dedicated band of volunteers for no pay and little thanks. Sometimes there are only a handful of riders and fields rarely exceed 20 or so.

One of the great benefits of living where I live is the access this affords to lots of midweek time trials. I once worked out that I could race four nights out of five if I wished. My own club promoted Wednesday night events, but I could race on other days without a drive of more than 30 minutes. I regularly did this, particularly in my early days as a returnee to the sport. You might imagine I made lots of friends doing so, but no, I didn't; I just met lots of people who treated me with the same standoffishness I received at my own club. It's not a criticism, by the way; it always made me feel vaguely at home. At least I always knew what to expect.

Preparation for midweek evening events was always a challenge. I would leave my car parked strategically at the nearest railway station ready for a last-minute dash out of London, picking up some pre-race food on the way. This would be followed by a short drive to that evening's venue with only a few minutes to spare. I would always try to warm up after stripping off and changing into my cycling kit in the car. As I always do this in laybys, I am frequently concerned about the police turning up, thinking I'm preparing myself for an evening of dogging or some similar car-based sexual encounter. Luckily that hasn't happened – yet!

The club time warp

One of the great things about competing in my own club's time trials is the various competitions and therefore trophies available to win during the season. I set out with no aim to achieve any trophy in my first season back and indeed my second. But I soon found myself leading the club's handicap 10 competition. This is a season-long competition comprising ten 10-mile time trials over various local courses. In each event participants score points based on their handicapped place in the time trial. The handicap given to riders is based on their best time over 10 miles in the previous year's club events. Due to my awful times set during my first year back I became the cycling equivalent of a so-called golf bandit: those who play way better than their handicap suggests and then walk away with all the prizes.

I led the 2011 competition from the first event and in the end all the way to the completion of the series. After the first two or three events I hadn't really noticed but then it was pointed out to me that I could win it if I carried on. I did have some immediate issues as I knew there would be at least two qualifying events that I wouldn't be able to ride due to holidays. The pressure was on; all of my own making, I add.

What I didn't realise at the beginning was that every time I beat my earlier performance I made it more difficult to 'win' on handicap next time, as my new handicap reflected my faster time. I quickly worked out that there had to be some tactical riding: just going fast enough to take maximum points but leaving some 'in the tank' for the next time. It wasn't all that easy as there were many riders pushing for the number one slot and towards the end of the season I did leave myself a lot to do.

A 30-YEAR CYCLE

In the end, I was a clear winner of the competition and although it was down to some good performances and improvements I also benefited from being able to ride in eight out of ten events, more than most. I would even turn out in all kinds of conditions, knowing some would probably not turn up. For the first time in 30 years I won something through riding a bike and it was a very nice trophy too.

At that year's annual dinner I was presented with my trophy and it was immediately mentioned that no one had ever won the event in two consecutive seasons. I made a mental note to make that an objective for the following year. As it turned out I had left myself a mountain to climb; bearing in mind my improvement in

25-mile handicap cup – Newbury Road Club, 2012.

times over this distance, I was no longer a 'bandit' and I had to really improve to score points.

After a couple of events in the 2012 season I was nowhere, with only a few points. It wasn't until later on in the season that I realised I was in with a shout, but by then I had run out of events to ride and again holidays took their toll. I managed to finish third. If I had had more confidence in my ability to improve and focused on the handicap competition, then I might have won again. My main focus, however, was improving my 25-mile times, so the handicap 10 competition was a bit of a side show in any case.

I did still manage to win a trophy though, this time a one-off handicap event over 25 miles, by about eight seconds – a close one, but as they say, a win is a win! Although I had no expectation of winning anything, it showed that for me, as soon as there was a sniff of a win, the old competitive instincts kicked in. I was a bit embarrassed that all I could succeed in was events based on handicap times and took a fair bit of piss-taking about this, but only of course from those who won nothing!

So that's the club scene. I see it as politely resistant to change and full of characters, some with very similar traits to those I was around 30 years ago. I feel at home with them and proud of this very British heritage.

Training then and now – power to the people

The A34 has dominated my life. I was born just a few miles from it, south of Stoke-on-Trent, in the days when expectant fathers didn't accompany their wives into labour. I am still quite sad, after witnessing the birth of both my sons, that my own father was denied that pleasure, even though he, unlike me, wouldn't have been fascinated by the gory bits and certainly would not have cut the umbilical cords.

For most of my early life I lived very close to the A34 in Stafford and many of my bike training rides, especially the chain gangs, were on the A34.

Admittedly, I had a few years away, living in London, and then it was the A24 and briefly the A5 that were my local 'trunk' roads, but when the move out of London came, it was to a village south of Newbury and, wait for it, close to the A34 again. These days, however, no cyclist in their right mind would take a bike on what is now virtually a motorway, certainly on the stretches near me, being an arterial north-south route.

Even one of the fastest time trial courses in the UK, on the A34 just north of Newbury where Chris Boardman achieved his 25-mile record, is now disused due to the high traffic count. I only wish I had been around in the sport before that course was banned due to dangerous traffic levels.

Training then and now

Away from the main roads, my training time was mainly spent on Staffordshire country lanes and one in particular.

They are still there. The telegraph poles I chalked with numbers 1 to 6 in Long Lane in Dunston, near Stafford, where I used to do my interval training. Ladder sprints, to be exact. The first sprint was between two telegraph poles, building up, in increments of two telegraph poles, to a 12-pole sprint. Then I would start all over again and do this routine between three and five times before cycling home at a leisurely, warm-down pace.

One of my first real attractions to a girl came about while I was doing my ladder sprints. She would regularly ride her horse along the lane as I pedalled furiously one way and then ambled back. We always acknowledged each other and would talk briefly if I was on the easy ride

Long Lane in Staffordshire – where I did my ladder sprints. The telegraph poles are still there.

A 30-YEAR CYCLE

to start again. Alas, though, I never summed up the courage to take it any further. If I was sprinting at the time she came past I would ease off and touch the brakes in deference to her horse, but we would then only give each other a brief nod. She probably thought I was some kind of deranged weirdo anyway.

The rest of my training was just putting in the miles, either on my own or with my then training partner, Andy. I would also go on the twice-weekly chain gangs and occasionally ride a midweek time trial over 5, 10 or 25 miles. In the height of summer I competed in the track league at Wolverhampton's Aldersley Stadium and sometimes at Halesowen and Salford in Birmingham too.

Keeping up with the chain gang was a real badge of honour at the time. It took me a few weeks until I could manage it. At first, like a few others, I was 'blown out the back' in the first few miles. Eventually I would come to be a dominant force in the group unless one or more of the club's first category riders came along, and then I would be firmly put in my place – at the back, biting the handlebars while fighting to stay in contention and avoid being 'dropped'.

To me, and I guess every cyclist, there is nothing worse than getting dropped by the person or group you are riding with, whether it is socially, in training or certainly while racing. It is the ultimate humiliation. No one ever talks about it; there are just knowing looks. If it's you, then you know full well if you are inferior.

I say there's nothing worse, but that's not entirely true: one thing that can be even worse is if the group then slow down or even stop and wait for you. They don't do this if it's a race, of course, and in many ways that's better. On the occasions it's happened to me I've often felt that it would be better if the ground had opened up

Training then and now

and swallowed me rather than leaving me to face the acceptance that I am the weak link in a group.

There is only one cyclist I know who doesn't seem to worry about any stigma of being dropped: Stuart. He only used to come out infrequently but when he did, regardless of the weather, the terrain or pace he was always happy. He would often get dropped on hills or even the flat when the pace was forced. We would wait for him and he would roll up five minutes or so later, pushing an enormous gear, smiling and commenting on how wonderful cycling is. If it had been me I would have been pissed off and thought *fuck this for a game of soldiers*, but not Stuart – I christened him the happiest man on a bike!

Our 1980s chain gangs only had two routes: a circular trip around Wolverhampton and Cannock, or Stoke and back. The latter ran on Tuesdays from Stafford, going north up the A34 to the Hanford Roundabout in Stoke-on-Trent and back. The route took you along a fast dual carriageway with only one real climb: Yarlet Bank on the way home. If you made it up there you had done it; after that it was a cruise back into Stafford.

Many Stoke-based clubs used the same route in reverse and occasionally the group would be swollen by other riders, making for almost road race-like conditions. Potteries-based club Tunstall Wheelers even had a following car, one of the riders' dads obligingly playing directeur sportif.

In those days there were only two things that you recorded while training: the time you left and the time you got back home. No cadence, elapsed time, power, average speed or the like.

Now, it's all about the numbers. You can regularly read quotes from those involved in coaching at Team GB

A 30-YEAR CYCLE

or Team Sky and they continually refer to the 'numbers'. Those numbers, of course, are mainly about the power that their riders can generate, measured in watts or watts per kilogram.

Training for cycling and many other sports has undergone a complete transformation during my near 30-year cycling wilderness period. In my youth, it could at times be fairly structured but nothing was monitored and improvement could only be measured by speed alone or ability to beat others. Now, it is clear that to ride 25 miles under the hour, a constant power output is required from the rider. A power meter can measure this during the event and also in training for the event.

Measuring power and heart rate is good, of course, but it does make for a different kind of riding. Every ride can be downloaded from whatever form of bike-mounted computer you choose to use. You can then keep it to yourself or share it with the world. I often see myself as a bit of an extrovert, but I like to keep my training and racing statistics to myself. Maybe if I was producing 400–500 watts over a reasonable distance I would feel differently!

Although most of my youth training was in either chain gangs or intervals, sometimes we would try other training routes. One was very close to my home, meaning I could get there quickly. Problem was this didn't allow for a real warm-up. The route was a circular one around a brand new housing estate, generally undulating and with one fairly steep climb. It was great for simulating a race but at that early stage the housing estate was not completely finished and on some sections the top layer of Tarmac had not been put down. This meant that some of the manhole covers in the road sat almost 50 millimetres proud of the road surface. There weren't many of them and if you were

Training then and now

on your own they could easily be dodged. In a group, however, it wasn't so easy. The new circuit proved to be a regular ride for us until one evening a manhole cover put paid to our enthusiasm.

One of the guys who sometimes came out was called Andy. He was a real poser: MG midget sports car and a brand new top-of-the-range TI-Raleigh team replica bike. The latter was the envy of many fellow riders as TI-Raleigh, as a professional team, were a real force to be reckoned with in that era under the guidance of legendary directeur sportif Peter Post. Also their bikes looked really smart in a bright red colour scheme.

Andy hit one of the manhole covers straight on. He and his bike flipped sideways and literally flew through the air before sliding along the ground. He had been right in front of me. I avoided the manhole cover easily but hit him. Brakes full on, the momentum raised my back wheel and, as if in slow motion, I began to realise my fate would be a journey over the bars. In a split second, I was brought back from certain multiple injuries by John, famously known as the Ayatollah, who had been behind me. He had managed to keep in control, and he coolly grabbed hold of my by now vacant saddle and tugged the bike back down. I didn't even fall off!

I never saw Andy on his erstwhile beautiful bike again and we didn't use that circuit again either.

Apart from monitoring heart rate and power, probably the biggest single change in training methods has been the advent of the turbo.

The turbo is an instrument of torture, the modern-day equivalent of the medieval rack, although of course the user is in control of the pain it can inflict. Basically, if it's not hurting it's not doing you much good!

A 30-YEAR CYCLE

The nearest training tool we had in my youth was a pair of rollers and even though they were useful for warming up and recovery, without any resistance they were too easy to give a decent workout. In addition, they required a certain skill to remain on them. One of my mates was using his in his mum's kitchen one evening, got carried away and bounced off the rollers travelling at whatever speed he had been doing on them. He hit the fridge and left a massive dent in the door, writing it off. It must have been interesting completing the claim form for the house contents policy, I'm sure.

At least with the turbo you are locked in and are going nowhere, no balancing skills required either.

My shiny new turbo arrived and I couldn't wait to get it out of the box. To my surprise it came with a free training video. Desperate to try it out, I set it up in front of a TV in a spare bedroom: mistake number one!

I climbed aboard and started pedalling, running up and down through the gears. It was amazingly realistic; the harder I pedalled the greater the resistance. I was surprised how hard it was to ride much above 18–19 mph.

I flicked the video on. This was a film of a race; a camera had been fixed to one of the competitors' bikes and the general idea was to try to keep up, riding at the same pace. Fuck, I thought, it's a criterium, never was any good at those, sprinting out of corners and all that.

I desperately tried to follow the 'race' and the instruction given by the commentator, but it quickly became obvious that I just couldn't do as he asked; I was at maximum effort. Had it been for real, I would have been dropped on the first lap – no change there, then!

What I hadn't planned for was the sweat generated by my efforts. My clothes and the carpet all around me were soaking. My shorts in particular felt as though I had wet myself. Then my elder son burst into the room only to tell me the noise of the video commentary and the whirring of the turbo had disturbed the rest of the house. They couldn't hear the TV downstairs.

I left the turbo alone for a while, quickly regretting the couple of hundred quid I had forked out. In time, however, it became a very useful tool and now I use it extensively to train when it is dark or wet, snowy, icy, or just for convenience. There are no punctures (well, most of the time; I have had one from a worn-out tyre), no other vehicles to contend with. It's as easy as slinging your leg over the saddle, hitting the right button on the computer and you're off.

What always happens with the turbo is that you get hot. Some people use a fan; some, like me, train in a near-naked state even with the garage door open. My milkman probably thinks I am a real weirdo. He regularly turns up when I am training in the early morning. I probably look like some kind of naturist who self-flagellates on a bike in skimpy Lycra shorts.

I often try to pass the time on the turbo by listening to music or podcasts. This really works for me on long sessions, especially when due to bad weather the time spent could be two or even three hours – yes, I do that regularly! Luckily, though, for shorter sessions, which often include intervals or at least some changes of pace, I don't find I need anything to help pass the time. The pain or even the concentration required to count the time of each interval is enough to help the time pass unnoticed.

For some reason, unlike many, I am able to switch off and sit in my garage pedalling away for what feels like endless sessions on the turbo. The view is always the same; sometimes it is cool, sometimes hot. In the summer, if I have time, I move into the garden. When I have my bike and turbo with me while on holiday, I set up somewhere convenient.

On one trip, a skiing holiday, most days I would get up well before anyone else and head to the garage for a session on my beloved turbo. The only good thing, bearing in mind it was unbelievably cold at times, was the view. As the sun came up there was a fantastic panorama in front of me of snow-clad mountains. I enjoyed that. Problem was that on a few of the mornings it snowed and the white stuff kept blowing into the garage – not very pleasant.

One of my ways of lessening the monotony of long turbo sessions has been to invite a few friends around. One snowy Sunday we had eight guys in our garage. I rigged up a TV for some cycling videos and downloaded some suitable music. We even had a virtual 'café stop' halfway through and my wife baked some fresh cakes. We managed three hours in total that day. The temperature in the garage went up from 3 to 16 degrees with condensation dripping off the ceiling!

What I hadn't anticipated was what the combined sweat of eight guys would do. The floor was as slippery as an ice-rink afterwards and needed to be swept out; luckily there is a drainage channel immediately outside the garage door.

Comments on the turbo aside, this is not a training book, but I am sure some could be interested in the actual training I do.

Right after I took up cycling again and before any coaching input, I tested out how fast I was by riding flat out over both 10 and 25 miles. I then set some milestones based on the sub-hour target for 25 miles, including how fast I would have to go in miles per hour. My performances from my initial time trials gave me a benchmark, but in the early days I also used to do 10-mile time trial simulations on the turbo.

My turbo time trials were like hell on earth. I only did them if I was unable to go out on the road for some reason; they did help break up the boredom of a long turbo session but boy, did they hurt – way more than the real thing! I would normally warm up for 20 minutes or so and then put the bike up a gear or two and go for it. Sweat would pour off me in buckets as my whole body screamed with pain. At first, the best time I could manage for 10 miles was over 34 minutes. The best I ever managed on the turbo before giving up this particular form of torture was 28 minutes or so, and at the end I was in such a state I could hardly climb off the bike. When I did, my legs buckled and I had to hold on to something to keep myself upright. By contrast, on the road, I could cover the equivalent distance in 24 minutes without anywhere near the same degree of pain and discomfort.

You may think, in view of my ability to suffer so much, I should be able to go even faster on the turbo, but as those who use one will know, you don't get the benefit of tail winds and undulations on a turbo. On the road, the weather conditions and the terrain can be used to your benefit. The turbo is just relentless; it's you against a machine cleverly providing resistance to simulate riding for real.

It wasn't until I started to focus on training with a coach and also use a power meter that any real progress came about. After a few months of DIY training, I trained with a programme written for me and used the power meter to measure my efforts and my improvement. I

A 30-YEAR CYCLE

seldom raced with my power meter fitted, though, and would just focus upon the average mph I needed to maintain. In view of this, I would often ride myself into the ground, pushing a big gear with my average speed dropping as the miles ticked away, and yet again record a poor time.

I really thought big gears would be my salvation. As my cardiologist had said, 'What you have to remember is that it's like your engine is governed.' The theory, therefore, was to develop more strength in my legs and ride at low cadence with a big gear on the basis that I wouldn't cope with high-cadence pedalling. I followed this idea for a whole season. It got me closer to my sub-hour goal, but then I seemed to hit a brick wall; I just couldn't go any faster. Even weight training had no effect in creating more leg strength.

Back in my youth I once managed, to the amazement of my friends at the time, to ride 25 miles in a time of 1:01:40. Not that great until you consider I had done it on a junior gear of 86.4 inches. That means for every complete revolution of the pedals the bike moves forward by that distance.

I hadn't planned it; it was laziness really. Juniors, those riders aged between 16 and 18, had to (as they still do) to race with a restricted gear. After a race at the weekend, rather than change my rear cassette so I would have a bigger gear, I left it on. At the start I thought I would be constrained and post a slow time. But no, I managed to get my legs going and achieve what was thought to be a very creditable time.

Notwithstanding this, my usual way of riding time trials was to push a big gear. This was partly due to my observation of the great time trialists of the day, who often used enormous gears, and probably a reaction against having to ride a restricted gear in road races. In time trials there was no restriction so it was a free-for-all, regardless of age.

So when I came back to it all those years later, I immediately assumed big gears were the way to go.

As I have already said, it did work to a point. I used to grind up hills in the big ring with my colleagues spinning beside me and also pushed my way along flat time trial courses. I soon tired, though, and it also caused my knees to hurt, not usually at the time but certainly afterwards.

So my pushing and grinding phase got me to three minutes over the hour. I would focus on my power output and if it dropped I would try to increase it again by going up a gear and pushing harder. Problem was I often couldn't push hard enough; either the strength wasn't there or I quickly became fatigued so I usually went slower.

After a couple of seasons and upon the advice of another coach I tried a higher-cadence pedalling approach. I was very sceptical at first as I really thought that due to my heart valve's inability to cope with increased blood flow, pushing rather than pedalling was the best way.

What I noticed was that if I started slowing down with power dropping, say, on a slight incline in a time trial, if I lowered the gear slightly and upped the cadence my power would actually increase.

In time I went from an average cadence in a race of just around 70 rpm to more like 85 rpm. This tale clearly shows it is about pedalling, as it always had been in my youth. What I also now know about those who use large gears is that they have the ability to pedal them at the same higher cadence and, hey presto, that's why they go way faster than me!

A 30-YEAR CYCLE

I have lost count of the number of 1980s winter nights I would be in my nana's garage doing circuit training and lifting weights. My dad used to time me whilst shaking his head. He thought it was all a waste of time and I needed to focus on riding a bike. But no, the magazines and training books said 'do some winter gym work', so that was what I did. Who knows whether it had any benefit? I do know for sure it seemed to have no effect whatsoever on my weak upper body and spindly arms.

Fast-forwarding a few decades, I got talking to a young professional rider and he told me how he and his teammates spent time on building core strength through Pilates. My wife does that, I thought. So I made contact with her instructor, Sonja, a very impressively fit fortysomething who is also into bike riding.

I had a lot of intensive one-to-one sessions with Sonja, using her various weird-looking but effective Pilates exercise contraptions. These included one called the reformer and the more exotically named cadillac; both would have looked at home in a medieval torture chamber! A lot of the time, though, we concentrated on stretching. It was amazing how inflexible my body was; I couldn't even bend over and touch my toes at first. My core strength also improved and I still do Pilates exercises almost every day, with infrequent top-up sessions with Sonja. Many others can't see the point but I think it has really helped my posture on the bike, especially when down in the aerodynamic TT position.

During my initial training I used a certain book called *The Time-Crunched Cyclist*; I assume many people have used it as it is designed for people just like me who have little time to train. It didn't work for me, though, so I went to a coach who wrote a specific programme. This was always based on midweek turbo sessions and weekend road riding.

Even now with a different coach my regime is much the same. I generally train five to six days a week. This training is a mixture of what are called sweetspot, tempo and threshold intervals and longer endurance rides, depending on the time of year. It seldom exceeds seven or eight hours a week. In the winter I will train on a road bike. During the season most of my turbo training will be down in the TT position on my time trial bike.

Many people make their training up as they go along but I don't think that's the best way, especially when time available to train is fairly tight. You need to train as efficiently as possible and of course maximise periods for resting. It's nigh on impossible to get this from a book, so I think it's really worth investing in someone who understands your objectives and can write a plan for you.

The fundamental difference in training methods now compared to my youth is the much more clever use of time; it is clear that endless miles that were prescribed then aren't needed. Also power and heart rate monitors allow clear feedback on progress even for amateur riders. Try not to become a statistics nerd, though!

You are what you eat

I really believe you are what you eat. One of the best things I did when getting back into cycling seriously was have a consultation with a nutritionist. It was truly a life-changing moment and the advice related to how I needed to eat not only for sport, but for life itself. I learned a lot about what and what not to eat and that the diet I had adopted as a youth would have been absolutely fucking hopeless, for anyone competing in a sport at any rate.

I used to eat three Mars bars before I raced. Not the normal size, but the king-size ones. Thank heavens they didn't produce the really big ones you can buy now, as I would have probably thrown up, become obese or even diabetic, or all three!

My pre-race chocolate boost did often make me feel sick. If I was in a road race and some stupid head-case decided to attack from the start then I would find myself feeling the Mars bars in the back of my throat. Thing is, they probably only gave me an energy boost to get me through to the actual start and then a deep low afterwards, just when I really did need the energy.

In the few days before any race, in an effort to carbo-load, I would eat an amazing quantity of food. It probably wasn't all bad but some must have been downright awful. My dad convinced me that bread pudding was a good way to add in the carbs. Bless him.

You are what you eat

He religiously bought me a massive gooey slab of it every Friday. Sad thing is I became addicted to it. I now know it was a waste of time for anything but the taste buds.

On pre-race days I would push down so much high-carbohydrate food it would make me feel pretty bloated. I would also be so full that in the evening or the following morning there would be an explosion in the loo at some time. No need for any details but we all know what goes in has to come out!

I also used to eat just before exercise. Now, I always knew this was wrong, but the chain gang I went out with on a Tuesday and Thursday left at 6.30 in the evening. My mum and dad didn't get in until 5.30 so I would often not be eating until nearly 6 pm. There were only 15 minutes to eat a large meal and then leave. Luckily the ride to the start was mainly flat or downhill and the initial pace wasn't too fast. I just used to find getting down on the drops of my bars very difficult for the first hour or so, as my stomach was very full.

I well remember my first visit to a coach in about 1980. We talked about training, of course, but touched on other things such as getting enough sleep and also eating. He said very little, but what he did say I have never forgotten.

'Don't eat tinned food; it's no good. Avoid pork – it's the meat with the greatest fat content – and a crisp packet probably contains better nutrients than the crisps inside. Oh, and last but not least: eat steak and eggs regularly for protein.'

As an official coach, in my eyes he spoke with authority about these things and pretty much fucked up my diet for a few years. In fact, today I still find it hard to eat anything out of a tin, never eat pork (except bacon –

funny, that) and feel so much guilt when I eat crisps it's not worth the bother. I do eat steak but not that often, although eggs are a firm part of my diet.

I follow a fairly strict diet these days of complex carbohydrates with a regular intake of so-called 'good' fats and protein for recovery. I would recommend a visit to a nutritionist; it's amazing what you can learn. What I learnt was that I had been eating crap for years and while it might get me through a day sitting on my arse in the office (and even then I would probably fall asleep in the afternoon), it wouldn't help my cycling.

Problem is when you try to eat properly it is difficult. My wife finds it very annoying when I turn my nose up at some of the wonderful food she serves because it has white rather than brown rice, for instance. As in all things, it's a balance and I try to stick to the good stuff most of the time, definitely in the days leading up to a race. But for an easier life, I normally allow myself to eat 'rubbish' one day a week.

One of the times my disciplined diet becomes obvious to all is during the working lunch meeting. I always seem to get invited to a few. At the appointed hour, in comes the food: crisps, lavish sandwiches and many other delicacies. I often don't touch any of it and am renowned for my self-control in not dipping in. Some of my colleagues at work marvel at my ability to stop myself eating the biscuits in meetings or nuts and crisps at the bar. I do have to fight hard. I can sometimes anticipate what will be on offer beforehand or just have to be strong and eat later. Sometimes, though, I think *fuck it* and ram the crisps down followed by a plateful of sandwiches; it's always great entertainment for those there.

There are some things I do crave: egg custards, iced buns, black pudding, McDonald's strawberry milkshakes, to name but a few. I will have all of these things but only very occasionally. Black pudding is often a 'guilty' treat. I don't know why, really, bearing in mind it's low in carbs and high in iron, so not that bad for you. To most people, though, the thought of eating what is basically congealed blood is disgusting!

On the way back from a race, if I have done well and I come across the 'Golden Arches', I am drawn into the drive-through lane to get my milkshake fix. My younger son, who is also into bike racing, likes his McDonald's fix too. It's often his reward for doing well. What kind of a parent am I? One who is probably going to completely screw up his diet by making the 'carrot' for good performance a high-fat piece of reconstituted meat in a white bun.

In addition to the food, we enjoy the challenge of getting under the canopy of the drive-through with the bikes unscathed on top of the car. I pull forward slowly; he leans out of the passenger window to give the OK. I must remember as he grows up that when he needs an adult-sized frame the drive-through will become out of bounds or a very expensive and embarrassing mistake will occur.

One of the very positive things about riding a bike for me was that the weight I had put on over the years of inactivity almost literally dropped off. All my running didn't seem to have much of an effect, but through cycling the pounds or kilos just fell away. At my peak, I had been just over 100 kilos. At 'racing weight', I was down to 76 or 77 kilos. At first I carried on wearing the same clothes, but jackets looked oversized and trousers were baggy, having to be gathered around the waist.

Eventually I had to give in and buy some new suits; my waist had been reduced from 36 inches to 33. I could

A 30-YEAR CYCLE

also fit in suits I hadn't worn for years, including my first ever dinner suit, bought when I was 21! Shirts with more than ample material and baggy collars became an embarrassment and a whole new collection had to be assembled, this time with a 'slim fit' label.

I still keep all my old suits, in anticipation of a time when the wheels may be hung up in favour of a more sedentary life again, perhaps due to failing motivation or injury. Hopefully this is a long way off.

Amongst cyclists, of course, my new svelte figure very much fitted in, but amongst my peers and many friends I stand out as being skinny.

I have noticed that a lot of cyclists don't drink, especially the racers. They are completely teetotal. I'm not. But I'm not far off, apart from the odd binge which seems to be a regular theme with cyclists – even Wiggo admits to that!

I remember going to a club night and ordering a pint of Guinness. When I got to the table everyone was on soft drinks of one kind or another. I felt as though I was a poorly disciplined guy, verging on alcoholism. We were in a pub, however. What's the point of meeting at a pub when no one drinks? I thought. The next drink I ordered was orange juice, though.

At the end of the season, after very little alcohol all year, I normally do have a couple of big nights out. But they only comprise a few pints, maybe up to five. The next day I will feel shit, any yearning for alcohol quashed for at least another year. Sometimes, though, the company is good and I'm having fun. There is no race the next day and I still go for it.

Like many others I have experimented with various foods and supplements that can enhance performance, all legal of course!

You are what you eat

I read one article about the benefits of beetroot juice. That was it; I was straight off to the nearest health food store, returning shortly after with a mixture of beetroot-based drinks. One thing I had forgotten was that I didn't actually like beetroot. It had been one of my pet hates as a kid. Together with tomatoes, the dreaded beetroot was avoided like the plague.

I must admit, if I were told that tomatoes could aid my performance I wouldn't eat them. That would be too much. I really can't stand them, although perversely I can face tomato soup (as long as it's Heinz and not home-made) and of course tomato ketchup.

After an hour or so of cooling it in the fridge, I opened the top and took a swig from the small bottle of beetroot juice. The by now chilled liquid wasn't too bad but instantly I remembered the feared taste from childhood. I pressed on and actually came to like it. I even progressed to drinking concentrated shots – a small bottle at the same price as a 250 ml one, meant to be taken just before exercise. Now this was really disgusting but I persevered despite the almost instant gagging.

There are side effects, however: no evidence of bettered performance, but purple shit. I can cope with this. But when the pee also turns pink I am deeply uncomfortable. I always fear I have started bleeding inside. The reason for this concern is down to the fact this happened once before, but with no ingestion of beetroot juice. On that occasion I found out later, after a trip to the doctor's, that it was due to passing a kidney stone. I had been in pain for days but hadn't known why.

One thing I would seriously recommend avoiding is getting kidney stones. I only had a mild case, apparently, but the symptoms were some of the most painful I have endured. Basically, three or four days of severe and

A 30-YEAR CYCLE

debilitating pain in the stomach that started with a dull ache and a belief I was constipated. It was only when my pee turned pink that the pain receded and I went to the doctor.

I really wanted to know how on earth I had got kidney stones and it was put down to poor drinking habits when exercising. Pick up any advice on sport, particularly running and cycling, and it will tell you about the importance of hydration. I wholeheartedly agree. You don't want to experience kidney stones. Now that's an incentive to drink, if nothing else.

A lot of cyclists drink coffee; I don't. Not very often, anyway. If I'm not on the bike it makes me hyperactive and uncomfortable. I know there are benefits but I am never happy with an increased heart rate and it can also bring a migraine on.

Talking about the effect of an increased heart rate, in a drunken state many years ago I actually ate a bunch of roses on the table at a restaurant. I couldn't sleep that night. At times I thought my heart would come out of my chest. In the end I went on my early morning run even earlier and posted my fastest time ever around my training route.

I don't recommend you use roses as a supplement, though; from memory, they don't taste that good and probably aren't legal!

Wow, that hurts

I don't think a middle-aged man can be involved with a sport and not pick up injuries. Even at the tender age of 30 I was surprised by the onset of niggles often caused by doing something I shouldn't have. I regularly hurt my back, spending pounds with the chiropractor, and strained various ligaments, so I was using the services of a physiotherapist regularly too.

My time away from any serious sport meant I was not a customer of either of the above, but as soon as I started cycling I was in need of the physio's services again.

I have had my fair share of cycling-related injuries over the last couple of years or so. Most have been caused by falling off, so I have suffered the usual road rash and general loss of skin. I don't think I have been through a single winter without falling off at least twice on unexpected ice.

One of my injuries, though, was more than a little strange.

After one of my early 25-mile time trials, yet another crap time recorded, I set off to ride home only to have a very strange feeling in my inner thighs. Within a couple of miles it turned to pain. I could hardly pedal and even sitting in the saddle became uncomfortable. The 12-mile ride home took well over an hour and the relief of getting off the bike was overwhelming. Walking, sitting and generally moving around didn't seem to hurt. I was

A 30-YEAR CYCLE

perturbed by the question of what it could be. All I noticed was that my inner thighs were swollen, so much so I couldn't stand with my legs together.

After a couple of days, nothing had changed. I even started to think the swelling was the new look of my thighs. After riding another time trial the following Wednesday the pain came back, with a vengeance. I resolved there and then to see a physiotherapist the next day.

'So what have you been up to?' he said.

'Just cycling,' I replied.

'There is just no way you could have done that cycling; you have groin strain on both sides!'

We searched for reasons why I had groin strain. He said what I had was often a footballing injury but only on one side.

As I lay there on the treatment bench I suddenly had a thought.

'I was skiing last week and did a water jump.'

'You did what?'

I explained that on the last day of my ski trip, together with a few others I had done the water jump. This involved stripping down to our thermal underwear, climbing a small slope and then descending at speed to cross a long pool of water on skis.

'That's it,' he said. 'When you hit the water from the snow the increased drag would have put a strain on your inner thighs; you should have warmed up.'

I made it clear warming up had been the last thought on my mind at the time. My thoughts had been focused on not getting wet and making a clown of myself in front of the growing crowd of spectators.

At least then I knew why it had happened. Nothing to do with cycling, although clearly my two time trials had made the strain worse. The treatment that followed was a bit of deep massage and an application of ibuprofen gel to help reduce the swelling. Oh, and keeping off the bike for a few days. I soon recovered.

Migraines are of course not an injury but an affliction I put up with. I usually get one every three weeks or so. I still haven't worked out the triggers, but thankfully it's not the often cited cheese, which I love. I have almost overdosed on cheese and had no migraines, then cut it out altogether and had some humdinger headaches.

It's not chocolate either. I can eat large chocolate bars in one go and in particular a well-known triangular Swiss brand that sells obscenely large versions. The only side effect I get is the shakes from a sugar overdose and of course feeling sick.

It all seems to be down to stress. I can drink and eat pretty much anything, but when I get tired or sometimes push myself hard, the dreaded migraine rears its ugly head.

After leaving hospital post-heart op, I had a migraine almost every day, sometimes with a really bad headache and nausea which often led to vomiting, but increasingly, thankfully, just the front-end visual effects that are what I imagine could be created by taking strong hallucinatory drugs, and then nothing else.

I still get migraines but can go for up to a month without one, then get two over a couple of days or so. I have learnt how to manage them and carry on working or even cycling, but my performance at whatever I am doing at the time is seriously impaired.

At work, it is often a case of trying to put on a brave face, easy if there are no meetings but when having to deal with others it can be a real struggle. I have to work hard to focus and, if it's a bad one, sometimes leave the

A 30-YEAR CYCLE

room to throw up, returning as quickly as possible. Migraines are debilitating and not really understood by many; they think it is like a bad headache and can be battled through. It's not. It can totally wreck any hope of functioning for, in my case, up to three or four hours. Many more hours for some, and I hear stories about people being affected for days on end.

There are times I get a migraine when out on the bike. If so, that's it. I just plug on but give up worrying about keeping up. If I'm racing then it's basically all over. When one comes on during a race, depending at what stage, I'll usually press on. Sometimes it doesn't really dent my performance, although I often pay for it later, with longer-lasting ill effects. On the odd occasion it comes on at the start there is really no point carrying on. I used to, but wouldn't now.

The number of my races and rides affected by migraines every year is very small – but sadly my worst ones are often linked to cycling. It is worth the risk of bringing one on, though, I enjoy it so much.

Enough of that; I hear migraines get better, meaning less frequent and less violent, with age. That's one bit of the ageing process I'm looking forward to!

Luckily I have managed, so far at least, to avoid any more serious illnesses and injuries. One of my mates did break his collarbone while out on one of our group rides. I was second around a corner, heard a crash behind and turned to see poor Pete literally fly through the air and land in a heap on the road. The guy behind me had slipped over, Pete had hit him and that was it.

As Pete lay there in serious pain, it was obvious something was wrong. He asked me to feel around his collarbone, so I did. Immediately I felt the broken bones underneath the skin. That was it; he was off to hospital.

Wow, that hurts

It's sad, I thought; four middle-aged blokes can be out having fun and bang, the next minute one of you is down. Then you really do start to feel your age. We don't 'bounce' or recover quickly like youngsters.

My dad, the directeur sportif

It was a joke and we often laughed about it but actually my dad was my manager and therefore my directeur sportif as the Continentals would call it. He really had fuck-all knowledge about what we were doing, but when I was a teenager somehow we managed to navigate around a few racing seasons together. When I made the senior ranks and he didn't come along any longer, as I had my own transport, it wasn't the same. His absence wasn't the only reason, but I soon gave up.

One of the funniest things my dad and I contrived to do was always tell my mum I had made a top ten place. There was a good reason for this; my mum thought the whole cycle racing thing was a waste of a Sunday morning, not to mention a waste of petrol. But if I did well she seemed to be appeased.

My sister, who sometimes joined us, would of course soon let on to mum about the truth – therefore she became a sort of talisman or even motivator. If she came, I definitely had to get a top six place and therefore points.

Dad was always there on a Sunday morning despite a late Saturday night. In those days my parents were big into ballroom dancing and every Saturday would be spent foxtrotting, waltzing and quickstepping around the dance floor at the local Trentham Gardens ballroom. They didn't return until the early hours.

Before he passed away in early 2013, dad as an armchair directeur sportif was quite an expert on the sport and in the virtual reality afforded by the excellent TV coverage of the current day, avidly watched all the major cycling tours. He was, however, often distracted by the stunning scenery or would drift off to sleep. He was adamant that bike racing on TV could be very soporific, until the last 3 km anyway; he'd never miss a finish!

Without him in my first cycling 'career', I wouldn't have been able to race. He took me everywhere. Did I always appreciate it as a hormonal teenager? No. Did I feel like I let him down with my performances? Many times.

When I did well it was great, but most of the time I was an also-ran and the lack of sleep for dad and the cost of the petrol his car consumed made it hardly worthwhile. We once made an ill-fated trip to the Worcestershire village of Inkberrow for a road race – probably the furthest we ever travelled. dad seemed to have set a 100-mile round trip limit. This, of course, broke that.

'Have you seen how far away it is?' said dad.

'Oh yes,' I replied, 'about 50 miles.'

'And the rest – more like 70 or 80 miles.'

In the end it was a 160-mile round trip; the pressure to perform became immense.

Unfortunately it wasn't to be my day; I was dropped on the last climb. Luckily for me, though, there was a massive pile-up in the bunch sprint and nearly all those there came down. It looked spectacular on dad's cine film and must have been very worrying to him at the time because he thought I was in contention. But

A 30-YEAR CYCLE

no, I rolled in with a small group a couple of minutes down.

My best ever road race performance also got me a serious telling off. It had been a classic junior race. Two guys slipped away and the rest of us did bugger-all about it. Eventually when we did it was too late. They had a massive lead and the chasing going on at the front of the bunch was sporadic and without real focus. The best I could do was third place. I knew dad would be pretty unhappy with what had happened. As we came around the final corner, I found myself at the front of the bunch on the inside kerb. Without really giving it a thought, I just went for it, flat out. Before I knew it I was clear. I had no idea how far it was but we had already passed the yellow 'kilometre to go' flag so it couldn't be far. Finally the line was in sight; I was still clear but aware from the noise someone was coming up to me from behind. I just put my head down and powered on.

At last, I crossed the line just before I was caught. The rider in question was no less than the then national junior pursuit champion. He wasn't happy that I, an unknown, had beaten him. I was very pleased but dad was cross.

'If you lot hadn't let them get away you would have won.'

I just stood there still straddling my bike and slumped over my handlebars.

'You should have seen the two who came in first; they were all in and could hardly sprint.'

I am not so sure, actually. If the whole bunch had been together it may well have been different and my positioning in the final kilometre a little more difficult. We'll never know, of course. Third was good enough for me, in any case – it guaranteed enough points to go

My dad, the directeur sportif

straight from junior to a second category rider rather than start as a third category senior: one of my objectives of the time. But dad used to go on and on about what had happened.

We seemed to slip into a routine for these weekly events. I would nip out on the bike to loosen up on a Saturday and then spend the rest of the day preparing my bike. It's amazing and probably a little sad that this is a routine that would be followed nearly 30 years later, much to the disbelief of my wife. I always justified my time away racing at weekends on the basis that I would only be gone for three hours at an absolute maximum. In reality it took longer than that; doing an easy ride the day before, preparing the bike and then racing often took up much of the weekend. Combining that with my younger son's racing, many summer weekends are completely written off to two wheels. I fear I am becoming another 'Dad the DS'; luckily, though, I do have a better knowledge of the sport than my dad ever did.

Another moment with my dad was when I had the misfortune, but in many ways the luck, to puncture in the neutralised section at the start of a road race. All road races then and now have a neutralised section as a feature. There is no racing allowed in the first few miles, then the lead car pulls away and the race begins.

Anyway, we had only gone a short distance and I felt my rear tyre had gone flat. What happened next was really unfair on dad. As if my guardian angel was looking down that day he was following the race in his car. I stopped by the roadside; he pulled up. I shouted at him to get my spare wheel out and help me out. He did, but then it all went horribly wrong. I got my punctured wheel off the bike but he made a complete hash of putting the new one on. The truth was that he

A 30-YEAR CYCLE

had never done this before and had no idea how to change a wheel on my bike, let alone do it under pressure as the bunch literally pedalled away. We finally got it sorted, but I had a hell of a chase to get back to the race. I knew if I didn't make it back before the lead car pulled away it could be race over for me. I did and made it all the way to the finish only to be thwarted by the uphill sprint. As it was a fairly local event there was no need to invent a top ten place. My mum didn't appear to mind if we hadn't travelled far.

Dad was a great support. Soon after I had come over the line he would be there with a drink and a fresh grapefruit. Why grapefruit? Well, it was very refreshing, especially on hot days. I would devour what he hadn't already eaten together with a re-run of my pre-race food, a Mars bar or two or some bread pudding that he would buy specially for the event.

He would hand the food and drink over and then the race post-mortem would begin. This was always fairly brief, intense, very calm and all too often tinged with disappointment.

On one occasion, the support I needed was more than just food. This was after a so-called 'spring' road race in Albrighton near Wolverhampton. What had indeed started off as a very pleasant spring morning turned very ugly. Dark clouds formed followed by heavy rain and then shockingly a full-on snow storm. The road turned white as the bunch just went into a slow-paced survival mode, all of us totally inappropriately dressed in shorts, lightweight racing vests and fingerless mitts, not gloves.

Some of the guys who were obviously tougher than me contested a bunch sprint of sorts; I just wobbled over the line, soaking wet, shivering with my hands unable to operate my brakes. Nearly all the field of riders must have been verging on hypothermia. My dad caught hold of me and quickly gave me my tracksuit top. It helped a little but I was shivering uncontrollably. He led me to the changing room at the race HQ which fortuitously was nearby. I was so out of it with cold and not in control of my hands, let alone my fingers, that he had to undress me.

It was a very embarrassing experience. My willy had shrivelled up in the cold and had all but disappeared. I certainly couldn't feel it. I stood there shivering as my dad removed all of my clothes and pestered me to get something warm and dry on. Others around me just like little boys were being tended in the same way. Even when I was fully dressed in warm and dry clothes I couldn't stop shivering. The heater in the car on the way home blasted away to help my recovery. Looking back, it was a horrendous experience. I have stood shivering at the start of many races waiting for the off, wearing only a skinsuit and have ridden and trained in all kinds of poor conditions, but none as bad as that day.

We travelled miles, spent many pounds on petrol and overall it was a very poor investment in my sporting future with a big fat negative return. Even if I had raced for 30 years I don't think he would have achieved any form of payback. But it wasn't about that. Through cycling my dad and I formed a close bond that lasted well beyond our few years while I was racing. We were more than father and son, friends as well. My return to the sport in 2010 rekindled that bond. He may not have been as actively involved then, but was still a big part of it.

I never really asked but I don't think my dad had ever ridden a bike, let alone raced. He had been a keen sportsman in his youth, though, and to him it was

A 30-YEAR CYCLE

certainly not about taking part! He was only interested in winning. I let him down more times than I care to remember, but always did my best and still do, thinking of the times when he used to be in support.

Until he passed away, the first phone call I would get after a race would be him, asking about my time. Then he would quietly listen as I often moaned about another mediocre performance. When I did deliver, though, his joy was obvious but measured. I try to keep that in mind now when supporting my sons in their sporting endeavours.

Family matters but it doesn't matter to family

If you walked down a residential street and were then asked to identify the cyclist's house it would probably be fairly easy. I would look for the one that needed painting, with a drive that needed weeding and the grass on the front lawn looking a little long and unkempt. There would be no obvious signs of any DIY activity and on Sundays all would be quiet; the cyclist of the house would be unlikely to be in residence, away riding or racing.

Even in my youth I always had a feeling of guilt that my cycling activities got in the way of family life. My dad had to do without sleep and to spend money that could have been spent on family things rather than on petrol for long trips. When others were heading off on warm summer weekends to the coast, my dad would be standing at the roadside watching me fail to perform and my mum probably at home doing the housework.

I discussed this once with the sister of a national champion cyclist I used to race against. She told me that during her whole childhood the family never had a proper holiday. It all revolved around her brother's racing. So no great surprise she got involved with the sport too.

They say cycling is the new golf. I assume only due to

A 30-YEAR CYCLE

its current popularity. But they do have a few things in common. They are generally not family sports and lead to the participant being away for long periods, especially at weekends. They are also conducive to 'boys'' weekends away, but minus the alcohol for most cyclists.

Of course, cycling is far more strenuous than golf, although some players do try to make out they get a good workout walking around the golf course, and doesn't really have a social side to the same extent. The 19th hole in cycling is probably the kitchen at home, recovering with a protein shake, not a beer or gin and tonic in a smart 'clubby' bar.

Just as with golf and probably many other sports or hobbies, balancing participation in cycling with family life can be tough. The main way I have tried to redress the balance is through losing sleep. I nearly always train in the early morning and more often than not the time trials I ride allow me to be back home well before lunchtime. Sometimes, when riding local courses at weekends I have made it home before anyone else in the household has even got up. Problem is, as my wife often reminds me, I still spend hours tinkering or cleaning my bike in the garage and often fall asleep in a chair during the afternoon as I'm so knackered!

Time trialling is not really a spectator sport, so there's no point taking the family along. It just involves a long wait by those supporting you and then all they see is you flashing past (hopefully), head down and in a trance-like state of suffering. The trial itself is often seen as futile by my wife too, especially as I seldom seem to have a good ride and then spend inordinate amounts of time moaning, complaining and analysing the reasons why.

The way I have tried to get my family involved, apart from encouraging my two sons to race, and that has its

Family matters but it doesn't matter to family

problems due to conflicting events, is by arranging a sweepstake for them on my likely time. They can all have a wager on my performance and at least then are likely to ask how I did when I return home. But they aren't really bothered.

'Are you embarrassed with your time, Dad?'
'No,' I replied.
'Well, I am,' said Arthur, my then ten-year-old son.
I laughed and we pedalled quietly on.
I had just taken part in the Newbury Road Club annual hill climb championship, a 1.1-mile event up Walbury Hill in Berkshire. Hill climbing isn't my cup of tea, nor my focus, but I had been cajoled into taking part by Arthur, who wanted to see his dad perform, and various club members I know, who, when I turned up just to spectate, made it quite clear taking part was a must.

I feared embarrassment but decided to have a go, knowing at any rate it would only be a few minutes of pain and my entry would help swell the number of participants to eight! Dave the timekeeper had turned up as he always did and the least I could do to acknowledge his support was have a go.

The previous evening, when Arthur had announced he expected me to ride I had thought about the event and weighed up the pros and cons; yes, it would be over quickly and the result just as quickly forgotten, but there is pride and I knew it would be taking a knock.

I came in second to last. Problem with hill climbs is you have to just go for it, flat out, and that's when my heart can behave in strange ways. Basically it's my body telling me not to be so stupid and to behave like a middle-aged man with a valve replacement and not a teenager! But as it says on my Twitter profile I'm 're-living my youth on a bike' and that's what I like to do – backing off, of course, when I think I have pushed it too far.

As you can imagine, it's at times like that I really wish I had a normal heart and could really give it all I have got to show my prowess on a bike. But I always err on the cautious side and when sprinting uphill comes to mind I think about what that kind of effort can do to me. There have been many times when I have pushed myself right to the limit on climbs or even on the flat. The power is there and I can compete against the others. Only problem is that this kind of effort can bring on my atrial fibrillation and my heart races away at well over 200 beats per minute, which is not good.

It is sometimes frustrating, though. I might be passed by a cyclist or dropped on a hill. Most normal guys would just dig deeper and keep up. If I do that it can certainly ruin the day. I will sit up and swallow my pride; I have found it's all about playing to your strengths and acknowledging your weaknesses.

In the end, the only real embarrassment I felt after the hill climb event was to do not with my heart, but with the fact that my gear had been stuck in the big ring. What's embarrassing about that? Well, the fact it was all my fault and was a problem I had experienced a few times on that particular bike without sorting it out for once and all. I am normally meticulous about my bikes but for some reason had put up with this and in doing so let it come back to bite me when I really needed the small ring. I didn't tell Arthur about that, bearing in mind I am always telling him to look after and check his bike.

My older son Albert's main interest in my activities on a bike is basically to take the opportunity to beat me. He

Family matters but it doesn't matter to family

did a few times and I did get my own back but luckily he is more interested in rugby; I don't fancy having to keep on trying to beat a boy at his physical peak.

It's not just my family who don't get it. 'Get what?' you say. Well, they just don't understand why a 50-year-old bloke still wants to ride a bike competitively or at least at over 25 mph. My wife doesn't, even my dad (formerly my manager) didn't always get it and neither do most friends and work colleagues.

Many of you reading this book might not be surprised by this, although I think probably the very fact you are reading it suggests you are one of the few who would 'get it'!

The thing is, when you are amongst racing cyclists, even those of my age and, I hasten to add, even those substantially above, it is easy to be lulled into their world where PBs and winning do matter. For most of the population these things don't. Most are happy, and I say this as an observation, not a criticism, just to enjoy eating, drinking, sleeping in and life in general. They have no desire to push themselves. Some of them do, in their work or in helping others. Many would like to and occasionally give it a try, realise it hurts and promptly give up; very few really focus on a real goal.

But when you talk to the majority of people they soon make it very clear that they think what you are doing is weird and many ask 'what's the point?' I don't ever rise to this; I just laugh it off. In fact, I seldom talk about my exploits on a bike unless, as happens very occasionally, someone takes a real interest. Then I often find myself going into lots of detail about what I do. The person concerned either starts to understand or really begins to think I am just a sad, strange, obsessed, middle-aged guy.

A 30-YEAR CYCLE

Of my fairly close circle of family, friends and acquaintances, excluding cyclists, that is, I could count on the fingers on one hand those who do understand the objective I set myself and why I do what I do. Does this really matter? Well, no, not really. The only thing is I often find myself explaining my motivation for what I do. As time has moved on, however, I have increasingly tended not to bother.

It is refreshing when someone you talk to does identify with you. We all need that as human beings. Trouble is that when they do, I can go off into detail about it all. Afterwards, when we have finished talking, it feels like I have taken advantage of them and their interest in my endeavours, and pangs of guilt come over me in waves.

In fact, I only really know two cyclists who were interested in my objectives. I enjoy talking to them as, in their own way they, are inspirational. Both of course are much better than me. One of them gives performances that will remain well out of my reach, no matter how hard I train or how long I ride a bike. It's almost as if we are drawn together – like a magnetic force of cycling obsession.

Talking of the word 'obsession', my wife has long held the belief that I was obsessed, not only with what I wanted to achieve but also with cycling itself. Naturally, I didn't and still don't agree; that would be taking it too far. Admittedly, I did have to immerse myself in everything to complete this book, but fundamentally I train when I have to, rest when I need to and race when suits. Outside that I am a dad and husband. My hours at work take up far more time than riding a bike – I spend no more than eight hours a week on the latter, mostly, in the winter months anyway, while it's dark and they are all asleep!

It is nice to be asked how you have done, but does it

Family matters but it doesn't matter to family

really matter? I set my goal for me. Not anyone else. My family don't really give a toss whether dad does well or not when he races. Quite refreshing, really.

My conclusion is that the best thing to do is shut up, don't talk about riding a bike and just get on with it. I'm sure you agree! Or maybe you don't; you did buy this book.

Nearly there, nearly there

'It's going to be next year – you won't get any fitter now.'

Just the words I didn't want to hear from my coach. I knew he was right and I had been kidding myself I would still improve. It just doesn't happen when you get well into the season, though.

In the midsummer of 2012, I became very frustrated. My large improvements of the previous season had melted away. I could still turn in a good ride and better my PBs by a few seconds, but it was hurting a lot and I just couldn't see a way of reaching my sub-hour goal.

I toyed with the idea of giving up for the first time and actually talked to my coach, Adrian, and told him that was it. He was very understanding and made no attempt to persuade me otherwise. I think he was probably relieved and wouldn't miss my moaning about lack of progress on our weekly calls. For a couple of weeks or so I bumbled around trying different things and pushed myself very hard at times.

I remembered the words uttered by my cardiologist the year before:

'You will go under the hour, I'm sure,' he had said.

Wow, I had thought at the time. This was coming from a heart surgeon. I didn't believe it. All the other consultants with a similar specialisation, and indeed doctors in general, had dismissed my plan. One fairly 'old-school'

Nearly there, nearly there

heart specialist had told me I should be grateful to be alive and just enjoy a sedentary life!

My cardiologist's assurance alone gave me a real drive to stick to my guns and keep trying.

Then, by chance, I stumbled upon a coach on the web. On my daily commute, I have nearly an hour on the train, sometimes longer when points have failed, engineering works have overrun, cables have been stolen or someone has decided to end it all at Wimbledon; it has taken me up to four hours to get home. I use the train time to good effect, sometimes working but often idly surfing the web. It was during one of these sessions that I came across John. He specifically concentrated on coaching people for time trials and seemed to offer a straightforward and low-cost approach.

I sent an email to John. To my surprise he replied very quickly. Within a few days and using a plan devised by him, I was back to structured training again with renewed vigour.

My new regime allowed for more rest and a lot less racing, but some very hard training sessions. I didn't like it at first. I missed racing every weekend as for some reason I liked to have the competitive 'fix' of a race, but it was the training sessions I found especially tough. I had done lots of hard work before but these were brutal, basically all flat-out intervals at what is called threshold. That's the maximum effort you can sustain before the pain becomes overwhelming.

There were times when I nearly threw up over the handlebars, the sweat would pour off me and at the end I would stagger off the bike and collapse in a heap before forcing myself to eat. The only reason I could cope with these workouts was that they were only twice a week and luckily not every week.

A 30-YEAR CYCLE

People around me knew when I had threshold sessions in the training plan. The day or especially night before I was often irritable due to not looking forward to what lay ahead. Afterwards I was just plain tired. Colleagues at work would comment that I looked 'shagged out' – they were right.

There have been ups and downs on my journey and I expected this. Knowing hitting my target was unlikely took some accepting. I realised I needed to have something to keep me focused. That year's handicap 10 competition was out of reach. I just hadn't performed when needed (although I ended up coming a creditable third.)

I cast around for something I could shoot for and the club's 25-mile handicap competition looked like a possibility. It was, after all, my chosen distance and with a bit of luck I would be able to turn in a decent ride that would win it based on my handicap time, even if I didn't go under the hour.

In the end I struggled to perform, missing the target time I had set myself by about 30 seconds. But just doing enough to win on handicap.

The competition coming the evening after my 49th birthday and coinciding with my parents staying meant that in the few days leading up I had some late nights. Eleven pm is late for me, by the way! I felt tired but heartened when I checked the weather forecast on the morning of the event. All indications were that it could be a 'float night'. As mentioned before, this is when all the planets are aligned, so to speak. There is no wind and the air is less dense than usual due to a high-pressure weather system, both of which allow a smoother passage of cyclists along the road!

I left work early to race off home for a quick change

Nearly there, nearly there

and then off to the event. After a puncture in a race the weekend before and the debris on the roads from the almost incessant rain, I decided not to risk another puncture during a ride to the start but to take the car instead.

That night I was also responsible for the admin of the time trial: organising the signing on of riders, collecting entry fees and handing out numbers. Due to this, I had to be a late starter, riding with the fast boys. Therefore, I knew I would find it almost impossible to catch anyone in front of me and, inevitably, would get caught by some of those starting after me.

Mark, one of the guys I know well, was off a minute after me and unkindly said he would see me when he caught me at the five-mile point. That comment spurred me on but also made me feel dejected in equal measure. Mark did indeed catch me just before five miles but I held him in my view for another five miles, so he acted as a good pacer for me. The rules of time trialling don't allow riders to use another competitor as a pacer, riding in their draught, so I must add that he was a good 100 metres or more away in front!

I also resolved when Mark passed me that I wasn't going to let anyone else catch me and they didn't. As I came up to the turn at around 16 miles my average speed was 24 mph. Fast for me at the time and well over my target speed: 23.6 mph. I have to admit I backed off a bit. I was in a lot of pain, so this wasn't totally about taking it easy; I just wanted to have something left for the final five miles, when I knew there were a couple of nasty little rises that would hurt and probably lose me another 0.1 mph or so.

My average speed came down to 23.8 mph as I neared Hungerford but I still felt confident of sticking to

A 30-YEAR CYCLE

my target. Sadly, a car pulling out in front of me and two mini traffic islands to navigate in Hungerford cost me another 0.1, the first rise yet another. Before I knew it, I was on my target speed and feeling all in. The week before I had blasted up the same rise in a 10-mile time trial and paid the price as I teetered on the brink of atrial fibrillation and my heart raced away; it had taken me about a mile to bring it back to normal. Normal for me in these circumstances, by the way, is about 150 beats per minute. I hoped this wouldn't happen again.

On the subject of heart rate, I often used to tell my dad about my 150 bpm rate and he always looked shocked. In his view, the heart beating so fast is likely to lead to instant death. Little did he know my heart has beaten a lot faster than that!

I had a colleague at work a few years ago who always shunned any kind of physical exercise. He positively revelled in being told by our company doctor that he should 'enjoy life and just relax with a gin and tonic every evening'. This was the same doctor who said my heart murmur was all OK about three months before my operation and was sued some years later by another colleague for not picking up his prostate cancer symptoms!

This exercise-shunning colleague believed that all humans only had a certain quota of heartbeats; once they were used up that was it, time up and death occurred. If this theory is right, maybe some of us have more than our fair share, or more likely it's complete rubbish and he used it as a good excuse to lead a sedentary life.

Anyway, back to the time trial. With my average speed down at 23.6 mph the pressure was on. I knew I had to hold it at this pace and figured this should be easy as the last couple of miles or so were flat or slightly downhill. What I hadn't figured into my calculations was the easterly wind. There shouldn't have been one, but, as is often the case, forecasts were wrong and there I was battling into wind.

My speed dipped by another point and this galvanised me into raising my game. With only two miles to go it was time to throw everything into my performance. I clawed back a point and then was slowed down again by the slight drag to the chequered finish. In a 10-mile event I will often sprint to the line to use up the last bit of energy but after a hard 25 miles this wasn't going to happen, so I stuck in my highest gear and just rocked the bike from side to side in a major effort to get to the finish line. The seconds ticked away and I passed Dave, the timekeeper, for a time of 1:04:02. My target was 1:03:30 but I would have been happy with anything beginning with a 1:03!

I won the Burns Handicap Shield by a measly six seconds. I agreed with myself never again to back off in a time trial, unless of course the pain became overwhelming.

Looking back on 2012 I did have a pretty good year, improving my 10-mile time by quite a bit and my 25-mile time by a little. I knew I needed to give it another season but desperately needed a boost. So I took the easy option and entered a 25 on the notorious Welsh Ski Slope course in South Wales.

The end or a new beginning?

My bike computer showed five miles to go. I was slowing down and the pain of lactic acid building up in my legs was rapidly becoming overwhelming. I dropped down a gear; my power increased but it hurt too much. I moved up a gear again and just pushed the pedals around.

In my head I worked out that even at an average speed of 20 mph I would be finished in just under the hour. With my head bowed and gripping the bars I gave it all I could. The last stretch of the dual carriageway was a real drag. Finally, I made it to what I knew would be the last roundabout. There was no traffic and I pressed on, flat out. The road rose again, slightly more this time. I had to hang on and keep pedalling until I got to the slip road, then it would be a brief relief as I went downhill before a final sprint out of the corner to the chequered finish line.

The roadside markers showing the upcoming slip road appeared in my now-blurred vision. Three lines, two, then one and off I turned. I was pedalling more easily now down a slope. The final turn came up rapidly; no cars were to my right so I remained at speed and put in a final sprint to the line. I immediately hit the stop button on my bike computer.

58:44! I had done it; the pain of the last five miles melted away and I sat up, moved to an easy gear and

The end or a new beginning?

pedalled back to the race headquarters deep in my own thoughts. The immediate thought was that I should have gone faster. But I always think that! On the ride back, which took a good 20 minutes, I gradually became happier with my performance and for once in my second cycling 'career' didn't have to think about what might have been or if-onlys.

The thing about time trialling is that it's your own personal battle against the clock. Yes, you are competing against others but it's still all very impersonal. I arrived back at the race headquarters very pleased with myself but totally anonymously, put my bike away and got changed, handed my number back and got ready to leave. As I did so, one of my Newbury RC colleagues arrived. He had a start time hours later than mine. He congratulated me on my ride and said, 'You were just about the time I had predicted.'

We discussed how the wind was getting up and that wouldn't be good. He didn't seem that bothered – I would have been very nervous about delivering a good time in the by then very blustery conditions. The wind didn't bother one other person: national record holder and time trialist Michael Hutchinson, or 'Dr Hutch' to his fans. He broke his own record in a time of 44:46. An amazing 14 minutes faster than me!

What I had done gradually sank in; I nearly cried. I had promised to call my wife and my dad but I couldn't. I was completely choked. I had done it, achieved my objective, sooner than I had thought I would but it had still taken three years. Not on a tough course, in fact on one where a downhill section at the start and good roads were a big help, but it was under the hour. I knew from that point on I could push for further improvement on tougher courses.

A 30-YEAR CYCLE

As I began the drive home, the only radio station I could get in the car was a local one called Nation 80. It proudly only plays music from the eighties. What a stroke of luck, I thought; what could be more appropriate music to listen to than tunes that had been around the last time I had gone under the hour?

For 20 minutes or so, as I sped along the M4 towards home, I was in a nostalgic musical trance and forgot to call anyone; I seem to remember the DJ playing the Buggles' 'Video Killed the Radio Star', Supertramp's 'Breakfast in America' amongst others and one from 1981 itself: the Police and 'Every Little Thing She Does Is Magic'. I was sad when I finally lost clear coverage from that station.

Two hours later, that was it; my sub-hour quest was all over. I arrived home. Nothing had changed. As usual no one was particularly impressed. We had a barbecue with friends in the pleasant late summer weather and it was hardly discussed, but inwardly I was happy and the feeling went on for weeks while I thought about what to do next.

All I would like to say in closing is if you really want to do something, do it, even if others don't encourage you or don't understand – do it for you.

Postscript

That event pretty much ended the season for 2012. Try as I might, I couldn't manage to turn in any decent performances in the few remaining events. In the end I missed a couple. The motivation had gone, I guess, and focus was upon 2013 – my 50th year. I had a couple of weeks rest off the bike during which, to my wife's surprise, I only went out twice. Then it was back to training.

Glossary

Atrial fibrillation – an irregular and often very fast heartbeat. Not good!

Bernard Hinault – French professional cyclist and five-time Tour de France winner.

Brereton Wheelers – my second Midland club, based in Rugeley, Staffordshire. Still going strong.

Cadence – the number of pedal revolutions per minute.

Chamonix – a town in the French Alps. Probably the worldwide mecca for mountaineering with spectacular scenery and real mountain men.

Chris Boardman – former professional cyclist and Olympic pursuit gold medal winner.

Cleats – plastic clips on the soles of cycling shoes that clip into pedals. They replaced toe clips.

Club runs – a tradition of British cycling clubs. Usually held on a Sunday where members ride together for a café stop or lunch.

Col de la Forclaz – the last col before Switzerland on the road from Chamonix.

Col du Lautaret – a col that leads on to the Col du Galibier in the French Alps.

Criterium – a fairly short bike race often on a city or town centre circuit, normally taking an hour plus a lap or two. They are fast and hurt!

Cycling Time Trials (CTT) – the governing body for time trialling in the UK.

Glossary

Derny – a motorised bicycle used for pacing cyclists on the track – used in the Keirin.

Devil – a type of race also known as Devil Take the Hindmost. Riders start in a group and on each lap one or more riders last across the finishing line are eliminated until three are left, then it's a sprint for the win.

Directeur sportif (DS) – manager of a professional racing team, often a former professional bike rider.

Eddy Merckx – probably the best professional cyclist of all time, five-time Tour de France winner. My teenage hero.

Elimination race – see *Devil*.

Étape (du Tour) – a sportive run over the route of a stage (or two) of that year's Tour de France.

Float day/night – a day/night when the winds are light or non-existent and there is a high-pressure weather system with less dense air – both conducive to fast time trial times.

Francesco Moser – Italian former professional cycle racer who won the Giro d'Italia and World Road Racing Championships.

Heart murmur – a sound in the heart that can only usually be heard with a stethoscope and can suggest problems.

Galibier – a major Alpine col and where the Tour de France can be won or lost.

Giro d'Italia – the Italian annual stage race and probably second only to the Tour de France.

Groin strain – an injury to the muscles of the inner thigh, most common in footballers.

Hugh Porter – fellow Midlander and former professional cyclist with four world championship pursuit titles.

Keirin – now an Olympic event, originating in Japan. A motor-paced race on the track where the riders sit in the draught of the pacer, who gradually increases the speed until with two laps to go he pulls off and they sprint for the finish line.

Mangelwurzels – potentially deadly root vegetables.

Pau – a delightful town close to the Pyrenees which sadly has bad memories for me.

PB – Personal Best, the best time you have recorded over a particular distance.

Pilates – core body strength exercises.

Potteries – a nickname for Stoke-on-Trent.

Reliability trial – a predecessor to the sportive but more low-key, timed over a set course early in the season. One way racers test their fitness. Still held by some clubs.

Road race – a massed start race.

Rollers – an indoor cycle trainer with three rollers upon which you have to balance on your bike. Unlike turbo trainers they offer no resistance.

Sporting courses – time trial courses often based on a circuit and over variable, sometimes hilly terrain rather than the standard dual carriageway out and back course.

Sportive – usually a long-distance massed-start cycling event held over a set course against the clock. Not a race but some treat it as such.

Sweetspot – riding between tempo and threshold pace.

Team Sky – the British professional racing team that was set up to win the Tour de France in five years and managed it in three.

Tempo – intensive endurance riding. Quite hard but you can still talk, just!

Threshold – riding at or just below the point at which the pain from lactic acid build-up in your legs makes you stop!

Glossary

Through and off – where riders take it in turns to ride at the front of the group, the other riders saving up to 30–40% of their energy in the slipstream. Riders take their turn and then peel off and join the back of the group; each rider moves up one, working their way back the front again.

Time trial (TT) – the so-called 'Race of Truth'. Just you and your bike over a set distance against the clock and the elements. Love 'em.

Tom Simpson – legendary British professional cyclist who won one world championship road race. Sadly died on Mont Ventoux during the Tour de France in 1967.

Tour de France – probably the best-known cycle race if not sporting event in the world.

Tourmalet – an infamous Pyrenean col used in many editions of the Tour de France – nice bus ride!

Track league – a weekly race meeting, usually as a series at a local velodrome.

Turbo – a contraption that allows you to train indoors on your bike while going nowhere and sweat profusely.

Velo Club Ventoux (VCV) – my first cycling club, based in Stafford. Now sadly defunct.

Welsh Ski Slope – a time trial course in South Wales that starts down a big hill giving riders a boost and leads to many PBs.

Wiggo – the one and only Sir Bradley Wiggins who has been responsible, along with a few others, for bringing cycling into the mainstream and renewing interests in mods!

Lightning Source UK Ltd.
Milton Keynes UK
UKOW06f0655210713

214117UK00009B/14/P